MAR 0 8 2003

American Decades

U·X·L

1930·1939

Tom Pendergast
& Sara Pendergast,
Editors

U·X·L®

THOMSON
™
GALE

Detroit • New York • San Diego • San Francisco • Cleveland • New Haven, Conn. • Waterville, Maine • London • Munich

THOMSON
™
GALE

U•X•L American Decades, 1930–1939
Tom Pendergast and Sara Pendergast, Editors

Project Editors
Diane Sawinski, Julie L. Carnagie, and
Christine Slovey

Editorial
Elizabeth Anderson

Permissions
Shalice Shah-Caldwell

Imaging and Multimedia
Dean Dauphinais

Product Design
Pamela A.E. Galbreath

Composition
Evi Seoud

Manufacturing
Rita Wimberley

For permission to use material from this
product, submit your request via Web at
http://www.gale-edit.com/permissions,
or you may download our Permissions
Request form and submit your request
by fax or mail to:

Permissions Department
The Gale Group, Inc.
27500 Drake Rd.
Farmington Hills, MI 48331-3535
Permissions Hotline:
248-699-8006 or 800-877-4253, ext. 8006
Fax: 248-699-8074 or 800-762-4058

Cover photograph reproduced by permission of the Corbis Corporation.

While every effort has been made to
ensure the reliability of the information
presented in this publication, The Gale
Group, Inc. does not guarantee the accuracy of the data contained herein. The
Gale Group, Inc. accepts no payment for

listing; and inclusion in the publication
of any organization, agency, institution,
publication, service, or individual does
not imply endorsement of the editors or
publisher. Errors brought to the attention of the publisher and verified to the
satisfaction of the publisher will be cor-
rected in future editions.

Vol. 1: 0-7876-6455-3
Vol. 2: 0-7876-6456-1
Vol. 3: 0-7876-6457-X
Vol. 4: 0-7876-6458-8
Vol. 5: 0-7876-6459-6
Vol. 6: 0-7876-6460-X
Vol. 7: 0-7876-6461-8
Vol. 8: 0-7876-6462-6
Vol. 9: 0-7876-6463-4
Vol. 10: 0-7876-6464-2

LIBRARY OF CONGRESS CATALOGING-IN-PUBLICATION DATA

U•X•L American decades
   p. cm.
Includes bibliographical references and index.
   Contents: v. 1. 1900-1910—v. 2. 1910-1919—v. 3.1920-1929—v. 4. 1930-1939—v. 5.
      1940-1949—v. 6. 1950-1959—v. 7. 1960-1969—v. 8. 1970-1979—v. 9.1980-1989—v. 10.
      1990-1999.
   Summary: A ten-volume overview of the twentieth century which explores such topics
      as the arts, economy, education, government, politics, fashions, health, science, tech-
      nology, and sports which characterize each decade.
   ISBN 0-7876-6454-5 (set: hardcover: alk. paper)
   1. United States—Civilization—20th century—Juvenile literature. 2. United States—
      History—20th century—Juvenile literature. [1. United States—Civilization—20th cen-
      tury. 2. United States—History—20th century.] I. UXL (Firm) II. Title: UXL American
      decades. III. Title: American decades.
E169.1.U88 2003
973.91—dc21
2002010176

Printed in the United States of America
10 9 8 7 6 5 4 3 2 1

Contents

Reader's Guide

U•X•L American Decades provides a broad overview of the major events and people that helped to shape American society throughout the twentieth century. Each volume in this ten-volume set chronicles a single decade and begins with an introduction to that decade and a timeline of major events in twentieth-century America. Following are eight chapters devoted to these categories of American endeavor:

• Arts and Entertainment

• Business and the Economy

• Education

• Government, Politics, and Law

• Lifestyles and Social Trends

• Medicine and Health

• Science and Technology

• Sports

These chapters are then divided into five sections:

Chronology: A timeline of significant events within the chapter's particular field.

Overview: A summary of the events and people detailed in that chapter.

Headline Makers: Short biographical accounts of key people and their achievements during the decade.

❖ **Topics in the News:** A series of short topical essays describing events and people within the chapter's theme.

✛ **For More Information:** A section that lists books and Web sites directing the student to further information about the events and people covered in the chapter.

OTHER FEATURES

Each volume of *U•X•L American Decades* contains more than eighty black-and-white photographs and illustrations that bring the events and people discussed to life and sidebar boxes that expand on items of high interest to readers. Concluding each volume is a general bibliography of books and Web sites that explore the particular decade in general and a thorough subject index that allows readers to easily locate the events, people, and places discussed throughout that volume of *U•X•L American Decades.*

COMMENTS AND SUGGESTIONS

We welcome your comments on *U•X•L American Decades* and suggestions for other history topics to consider. Please write: Editors, *U•X•L American Decades,* U•X•L, 27500 Drake Rd., Farmington Hills, MI 48331-3535; call toll-free: 1-800-877-4253; fax: 248-699-8097; or send e-mail via http://www.galegroup.com.

Chronology of the 1930s

1930:   Karl Landsteiner wins the Nobel Prize for his work in identifying and understanding the interrelationship of the blood groups A, B, AB, and O.

1930:   Ford sells 1.15 million of its popular Model A cars.

1930:   **January 14** Jazz greats Benny Goodman, Glenn Miller, Jimmy Dorsey, and Jack Teagarden play George and Ira Gershwin's songs, including "I've Got a Crush on You," in the musical *Strike Up the Band* at the Mansfield Theater in New York.

1930:   **March 6** Birds Eye Frozen Foods go on sale in Springfield, Massachusetts.

1930:   **May** The first airline stewardesses take to the skies with United Airlines. Job applicants had to be single women over the age of twenty-one, under five feet four inches tall, and weighing no more than 115 pounds.

1930:   **June 17** The Smoot-Hawley Tariff Act sets the highest import tariffs (taxes on imported goods) in American history.

1930:   **October 14** *Girl Crazy*, starring Ethel Merman, opens at New York's Guild Theater. The musical features songs by George Gershwin, Walter Donaldson and Ira Gershwin, including "I Got Rhythm" and "Embraceable You."

1930:   **December 11** The Bank of the United States closes, taking with it the savings of more than 400,000 depositors.

1931: Lutheran churches across the country merge to form the American Lutheran Church. Congregationalists merge to form the General Council of Congregational and Christian Churches.

1931: The International Bible Students Association becomes the Jehovah's Witnesses.

1931: Nevada legalizes gambling and allows divorce for couples who have been resident in the state for only six weeks.

1931: Jane Addams wins the Nobel Peace Prize for her work with immigrants and the homeless.

1931: **March 3** "The Star Spangled Banner" becomes the national anthem by Congressional vote.

1932: Edwin Herbert Land, a Harvard College dropout, invents Polaroid film.

1932: *The Jack Benny Show* premiers on the radio; it runs for twenty-three years and then another ten on television.

1932: **July 7** The Dow Jones Industrial Average hits an all-time low of 41.22.

1932: **August 25** Amelia Earhart makes the first nonstop transcontinental flight from Los Angeles to Newark. It takes her nineteen hours and five minutes.

1932: **December 27** Radio City Music Hall opens at the Rockefeller Center in New York.

1933: President Franklin D. Roosevelt presents the nation with his first radio address, known as a "fireside chat."

1933: **May 12** Congress passes the Federal Emergency Relief Act, awarding the states $500 million in aid.

1933: **June 6** In Camden, New Jersey, Richard M. Hollingshead Jr. opens the first drive-in movie theater.

1933: **June 16** The first "hundred days" of the New Deal ends with fifteen major pieces of legislation in place, including the National Industrial Recovery Act (NIRA).

1933: **August** The Negro League plays its East-West All-Star Games, watched by 50,000 fans at Comiskey Park in Chicago.

1933: **November 9** The Civil Works Administration begins providing emergency jobs for four million unemployed.

1933: **December 5** Prohibition ends with the Twenty-first Amendment to the Constitution, which repeals the Eighteenth Amendment.

1934: **May** Three hundred million tons of topsoil are blown from the plains states as far as the Atlantic Ocean in the great "Dust Bowl."

1934: **June 6** The Securities and Exchange Commission (SEC) is set up to oversee financial markets.

1935: The first canned beer goes on sale in the United States.

1935: The first hospital for drug addicts is opened in Lexington, Kentucky.

1935: **April 8** The Works Progress Administration (WPA) is created. It will eventually employ eight million people in building works and public arts projects.

1935: **May 24** The Cincinnati Reds host the first major-league baseball night game, against Philadelphia. President Roosevelt presses a button in the White House to switch on the lights.

1935: **June 10** Alcoholics Anonymous (AA) holds its first meeting in a New York hotel. The name of one of its founders, Bill Wilson, is not discovered until his death in 1971.

1935: **August 14** The Social Security Act creates a nationwide system of old age pensions and unemployment benefits.

1936: The U.S. Supreme Court hears the case of *Murray v. Maryland*. It rules that Maryland Law School should admit African American student Donald Murray or build a segregated law school. The law school admits Murray.

1936: **March 1** The Boulder Canyon Dam (later the Hoover Dam) is completed. The reservoir it creates, called Lake Mead, is the largest reservoir in the world.

1936: **August 2–9** Jesse Owens wins four gold medals at the Berlin Olympics.

1937: The first evidence of a link between cigarette smoking and lung cancer is observed.

1937: Wallace Carothers of Du Pont invents nylon.

1937: Dr. Seuss becomes a popular children's book author with the publication of *And to Think That I Saw It on Mulberry Street*.

1937: *Snow White and the Seven Dwarfs*, the first feature-length animated film, is presented by Walt Disney.

1937: The first soap opera, *Guiding Light,* is broadcast. It would continue as a radio program until 1956 and be seen on television from then into the early twenty-first century.

1937: **March 15** The first modern blood bank is set up at Cook County Hospital, Chicago.

1937: **March 26** William H. Hastie becomes the first African American federal judge.

1937: **May 30** Chicago police open fire on a union picnic of Republic Steel workers. Ten are killed, and eighty-four are injured. The event is known as the "Memorial Day Massacre."

1937: **June 22** Joe Louis begins his long reign as heavyweight champion when he knocks out Jim Braddock at Comiskey Park, Chicago.

1938: Birth control is legal, except in Connecticut, Mississippi, and Massachusetts.

1938: Orson Welles' radio broadcast of H. G. Wells's science fiction novel *The War of the Worlds* is believed to be a serious announcement of a Martian invasion by listeners and panic spreads throughout the country.

1938: **May 26** The House Un-American Activities Committee (HUAC) is established.

1938: **June 15** The Fair Labor Standards Act limits the work week to forty-four hours. After that, overtime pay is due to workers. A minimum wage is set at 25 cents per hour; 12.5 million Americans are affected by these changes.

1938: **October 22** The first "xerox" copy is made by Chester F. Carlson. His copying machine uses a process called xerography.

1938: **December 12** The U.S. Supreme Court orders the state of Missouri to provide equal education for African American law students.

1939: The General Electric Company introduces fluorescent lighting.

1939: The electronic instrument firm Hewlett-Packard is founded.

1939: *Gone with the Wind,* the epic film about the Civil War, starring Vivien Leigh and Clark Gable, opens in theaters.

1939: *The Wizard of Oz* whisks movie audiences into a fantasyland of magic and wonder. The film stars Judy Garland and includes such popular songs as "Somewhere Over the Rainbow," "Follow the Yellow Brick Road," and "We're Off to See the Wizard."

1939:   Little League baseball begins in Williamsport, Pennsylvania.

1939:   **May 2** Baseball star Lou Gehrig ends his fifteen year consecutive game streak when he withdraws from the New York Yankees' starting lineup.

1939:   **May 10** After 105 years of separation over the issue of slavery, the Northern and Southern Methodist Churches reunite. The newly named Methodist Church becomes the largest Protestant church in the United States.

1939:   **June 26** Pan-American Airways begins the first transatlantic passenger air service.

1939:   **September 14** The first mass-produced helicopter, designed by Igor Sikorsky, begins test flights.

The 1930s: An Overview

The Great Depression touched every aspect of American life during the 1930s. Millions of ordinary Americans suffered huge losses. After the 1929 stock market crash and the closure of hundreds of banks, people lost their jobs, their savings, and their homes. Some ate dandelions, ketchup, and even grass, because there was nothing else. In Washington State, homeless men started forest fires, then offered themselves for hire to put them out. Farmers in Kansas and the central states saw their land turn to dust, then blow away during what became known as the Dust Bowl. Where schools did not close, teachers often went unpaid.

With thirteen million unemployed, and millions more working reduced hours for lower pay, many Americans lived on the edge of starvation. Yet for the rich, life continued much as before. While the economy struggled, improvements in technology meant better transportation, improved medicines, and refrigerated food. Despite unemployment and record levels of homelessness, in science, sports, the movies, literature, and music, the United States saw a number of successes. By mid-decade, there were two nations, rich America and poor America. After the inauguration of President Franklin Delano Roosevelt in 1933, New Deal government policies set about healing the divisions. For all its faults, the New Deal gave Americans a focus and a sense of purpose that was lacking in Europe, which also was gripped by economic troubles. Perhaps because of this, the United States avoided the political turmoil that led to war in Europe in 1939.

Critics of the set of federal programs known as the New Deal complained about the growth of federal power and "communistic" welfare reforms. But the New Deal had a broadly positive effect. If nothing else, it brought together hostile interest groups such as financiers and labor unions. While some New Deal programs often seemed badly thought out and antibusiness, they were very popular. Although much of the success of the New Deal was due to good fortune, it was the Democrat policies of the 1930s that prepared the United States for the new economics of the post-World War II world.

By 1933 a new national culture was beginning to emerge. With the help of New Deal measures, ethnic Americans began to change the business environment. American culture began to refashion itself as inclusive, diverse, and multi-ethnic. Composers such as George Gershwin and Aaron Copland brought American folk music to the classical concert hall and the opera house. While the huge success of blonde-haired, blue-eyed actress Shirley Temple suggests that the old order lingered on, the United States ended the 1930s a more tolerant, less exclusive place. The new national culture made Americans more aware of their importance in a diverse and vibrant culture. This meant that Americans felt more a part of a group or community. They became more willing to join labor unions, and protest against unemployment and racism, and they saw their own struggles as part of the nation's battle against economic collapse.

In the 1930s, economic planning, social reform, and technology all made huge improvements to American society. Sulfa drugs were a major advance in the treatment of infectious disease, while high-speed X-ray machines made tuberculosis easy to diagnose. Health care improved with blood typing, transfusions, and improved anesthetics. Faster airplanes made long-distance travel easier, while the Boulder Dam showed the skill of American architects and construction workers. Genetic research became possible in the 1930s, as did atomic physics. The forward-looking spirit of the age was expressed through the "streamlining" of objects from automobiles to pencil sharpeners. The 1939 New York World of Tomorrow Fair offered a luxurious future of televised entertainment and work done by robots.

Americans ended the decade more sensitive to social injustice, more united behind the federal government, and more optimistic about the future. But as the Depression ended, war was already raging in Europe. World War II and its aftermath would dominate the next decade, and change U.S. relations with the rest of the world.

Arts and Entertainment

Chronology

1930: **January 14** Jazz greats Benny Goodman, Glenn Miller, Jimmy Dorsey, and Jack Teagarden play George and Ira Gershwin's songs, including "I've Got a Crush on You," in the musical *Strike Up the Band* at the Mansfield Theater in New York.

1930: **May 3** Ogden Nash, a poet who will become famous for his funny, light verse, publishes "Spring Comes to Murray Hill" in the *New Yorker* magazine and soon works at the magazine.

1930: **October 14** *Girl Crazy,* starring Ethel Merman, opens at New York's Guild Theater. The musical features songs by George Gershwin and Walter Donaldson and Ira Gershwin, including "I Got Rhythm" and "Embraceable You."

1931: **March 3** "The Star Spangled Banner" becomes the national anthem by Congressional vote.

1931: **June 3** Fred and Adele Astaire perform for the last time together on the first revolving stage.

1931: **July 27** *Earl Carroll's Vanities,* featuring naked chorus girls, opens at the 3,000-seat Earl Carroll Theater in New York.

1932: Edwin Herbert Land, a Harvard College dropout, invents Polaroid film.

1932: *The Lone Ranger* Western radio drama debuts.

1932: *The Jack Benny Show* premiers on radio; it runs for twenty-three years and then another ten on television.

1932: **December 27** Radio City Music Hall opens at the Rockefeller Center in New York.

1933: President Franklin D. Roosevelt presents the nation with his first radio address, known as a "fireside chat."

1933: **May 27** Fan dancer Sally Rand attracts thousands with her performance at the Chicago World's Fair that celebrated the Century of Progress.

1933: **September 30** *Ah, Wilderness,* acclaimed American playwright Eugene O'Neill's only comedy, opens at the Guild Theater in New York.

1934: The first pipeless organ is patented by Laurens Hammond. The Hammond organ starts a trend toward more electrically amplified instruments.

1934: **July 1** The Motion Picture Producers and Distributors of America (MPPDA) association creates the Hays Office to enforce codes that limit amount and types of sexuality and immoral behavior in films.

1935: **April** *Your Hit Parade* is first heard on radio offering a selection of popular hit songs.

1935: **October 10** *Porgy and Bess,* known as the "most American opera of the decade," opens in New York at the Alvin Theater. The music George Gershwin wrote for the opera combines blues, jazz, and southern folk.

1936: Popular public-speaking teacher Dale Carnegie publishes his book *How to Win Friends and Influence People.*

1936: To increase feelings of nationalism, the Department of the Interior hires folksinger Woody Guthrie to travel throughout the country performing his patriotic songs such as "Roll On, Columbia" and "Those Oklahoma Hills."

1937: Dr. Seuss becomes a popular children's book author with the publication of *And to Think That I Saw It on Mulberry Street.*

1937: *Porky's Hare Hunt,* a short animated cartoon by Warner Bros. introduces audiences to the Bugs Bunny character and the talents of Mel Blanc (the voice of both Bugs Bunny and Porky Pig).

1937: *Snow White and the Seven Dwarfs,* the first feature-length animated film, is presented by Walt Disney.

1937: The first soap opera, *Guiding Light,* is broadcast. It would continue as a radio program until 1956 and be seen on television from then into the early twenty-first century.

1938: Orson Welles's radio broadcast of H.G. Wells's science fiction novel *The War of the Worlds* is believed to be a serious announcement of Martian invasion by listeners and panic spreads throughout the country.

1938: **January 17** The first jazz performance at Carnegie Hall in New York takes place featuring Benny Goodman and His Orchestra, with Duke Ellington, Count Basie, and others.

1938: **November 11** Singer Kate Smith's performance of "God Bless America" is broadcast over the radio on Armistice Day.

1939: Singer Frank Sinatra joins the Tommy Dorsey band, where he will soon find great success.

1939: *Gone with the Wind,* the epic film about the Civil War, staring Vivien Leigh and Clark Gable, opens.

1939: *The Wizard of Oz* whisks movie audiences into a fantasyland of magic and wonder. The film stars Judy Garland and includes such popular songs as "Somewhere Over the Rainbow," "Follow the Yellow Brick Road," and "We're Off to See the Wizard."

❊ Overview

Despite the Great Depression, which gripped the country, the 1930s were an exciting time for the arts. Novelists such as William Faulkner, Zora Neal Hurston, John Steinbeck, John Dos Passos, James T. Farrell, and F. Scott Fitzgerald all produced major works in the 1930s. In the theater Eugene O'Neill and Clifford Odets wrote influential plays. In dance, jazz and ballet were fused in the work of Martha Graham. American painters and sculptors produced huge public artworks and began to move toward a more abstract style. Jazz, hillbilly music, and the blues found a broad audience in the 1930s, while the Hollywood movie embraced color and developed its own distinctive style.

Like nearly everyone else, artists, writers, and musicians suffered in the economic climate of the Depression. At such a time of crisis there was a sense that America had lost its way and that the country lacked a distinctive culture of its own. In an effort to boost national pride while helping to provide some jobs to help Americans through the Depression, the government's Works Progress Administration (WPA), one of President Franklin D. Roosevelt's New Deal political programs, supported regional artistic activity by giving federal funding to the arts. In many cases this meant that artists could continue to get paid to work when the market for their goods disappeared. The idea was not only to develop a modern American culture but also to rediscover one that was being lost. Artists, writers, filmmakers, and musicians traveled around the country documenting and borrowing from folk (common) culture. Some were paid to collect and develop the nation's regional art forms. Photographers such as Walker Evans and Dorothea Lange tried to capture the suffering of the poor, while many novelists tried to report the suffering by turning to journalism. Artists like Edward Hopper, Georgia O'Keeffe, and Charles Sheeler all used regional landscapes and scenes in their work, and in doing so, became closely associated with certain geographic regions of the country. Writers, too, were linked with the places they wrote about:

Nathanael West became known as a California novelist, while James T. Farrell was associated with Chicago, and William Faulkner with the South.

During the Depression the arts had to appeal to a mass audience in order to stay in business. There was no longer enough money to support work that did not sell well. In Hollywood many independent studios and theaters were forced to close, while the major studios turned to lavish musicals, thrillers, horror movies, and popular dramas that attracted larger audiences. Audiences looking for escape from their daily lives enjoyed child star Shirley Temple and her sugary brand of song and dance. Swing music, played by orchestras led by Count Basie, Benny Goodman, and others, entertained at dance halls around the country. Technology also helped make the 1930s an age of mass entertainment. The radio and the jukebox made drama, national news, and popular music accessible even to remote and rural communities.

In the fine and performing arts, the 1930s saw a conflict between modernists and traditionalists. The modernists looked to Europe for their inspiration and associated themselves with high culture. They favored experimental arts, such as abstract painting, music that lacked obvious tunes or rhythms, and novels without plot. Traditionalists focused on American themes and realistic images and associated themselves with what some called "low" culture. They reworked folk songs and retold tales of the West. Ultimately, neither "high" nor "low" culture dominated. Rather, the boundary between the two began to blur. From its beginnings as simple dance music, jazz, for example, grew into a mature and highly complex musical form. It became a favorite of middle-class urban intellectuals, as well as being popular with dancers. Writers such as Raymond Chandler and Horace McCoy wrote crime novels that were discussed as literature, rather than cheap thrillers, while painters such as Stuart Davis borrowed images from popular culture and advertising to create their otherwise abstract works. Across the arts the new national culture became one of mass entertainment, and popular Americana, showing a deep concern for the lives of "ordinary" Americans.

Thomas Hart Benton (1889–1975) The best known of the regionalist painters, Thomas Hart Benton began his career as a writer and illustrator for a newspaper in Joplin, Missouri. He attended the Chicago Art Institute and went to art school in Paris. Unimpressed with abstract art, in 1918 Benton began to develop a style he called "Americanism." Benton traveled widely in the United States, meeting and painting pictures of hard-working, straightforward, ordinary people. Benton's many paintings and public art works include a mural for the Missouri state capitol, completed in 1935. *Photo courtesy of the Library of Congress.*

Al Capp (1909–1979) Creator of the comic strip *Li'l Abner,* Al Capp was born Alfred Gerald Caplin in New Haven, Connecticut. His upbringing left him well qualified to draw and write about the hillbilly life of Li'l Abner. As the best-known comic strip artist of his generation, Capp enjoyed a celebrity lifestyle. But he kept on writing and drawing the strip for forty-four years. Capp's conservatism went out of fashion in the 1960s. After the comic strip was dropped by several papers in the 1970s, Capp retired Li'l Abner himself. *Photo reproduced by permission of Archive Photos, Inc.*

Joan Crawford (1904–1977) Probably the most adaptable actress of the 1930s, Joan Crawford was a major star of Depression-era Hollywood. She starred in romantic comedies such as *Forsaking All Others* (1934), gangster movies such as *Dance Fools Dance* (1931), Depression melodramas like *Possessed* (1931), and even an ice-skating revue, *Ice Follies of 1939* (1939). Crawford had a tough start, working in a laundry and as a waitress before being spotted working as a chorus girl in Detroit. Her career gradually declined in the late 1930s and she was eventually dropped by M-G-M in 1944. *Photo reproduced by permission of the Corbis Corporation.*

William Faulkner (1897–1962) One of the greatest American writers of all time, William Faulkner set most of his novels and short stories in the imaginary Yoknapatawpha County of Mississippi. He used the lives of a handful of fictional families to explore the history and society of the Deep South. The novels *The Sound and the Fury* (1929), *As I Lay Dying* (1930), and *Absalom! Absalom!* (1936) are among the finest novels of the twentieth century. Starting in the 1930s, Faulkner also wrote or co-wrote many screenplays, most notably for director Howard Hawks. *Photo reproduced by permission of Archive Photos, Inc.*

Ella Fitzgerald (1918–1996) Ella Fitzgerald's professional singing career began in 1935. She became one of the most successful vocalists of the twentieth century. In the 1930s Fitzgerald performed and recorded with the Chick Webb big band, but she also composed and arranged her own music. Her "A-Tisket, A-Tasket" was a huge hit in 1938. When Webb died in 1939, Fitzgerald became one of the youngest bandleaders in the country. In the 1950s, her *Songbooks* revived her career and made jazz popular again. As the unofficial "first lady" of jazz, she was still performing thirty-six weeks a year in the 1980s. *Photo reproduced by permission of Archive Photos, Inc.*

Woody Guthrie (1912–1967) Woody Guthrie, born Woodrow Wilson Guthrie, hitched rides, walked, and rode the rails around America during the 1930s. He wrote more than one thousand songs about his experiences, glorifying outlaws, outcasts, and the poor. Guthrie was also a political activist, writing for the communist newspaper *People's World* in the late 1930s. He became a big star in the 1940s but backed out of a contract with CBS radio because he feared "selling out." Guthrie's influence on American folk music can be heard in the songs of Joan Baez, Bob Dylan, and his son, Arlo Guthrie. *Photo reproduced by permission of Archive Photos, Inc.*

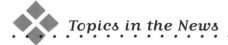

❖ THE GREAT DEBATE ABOUT ART

During the 1930s many debated whether quality art had to follow the trends set by European modernism or if it could be realistic and follow regional traditions. Modernist painting tended to be abstract, portraying feelings rather than scenes. Modernists saw people as alienated from each other and from the world. Many modernist painters tried to capture this feeling by representing the world as if through a distorting lens. Realistic painters depicted everyday scenes and people. Their works were certainly more popular with the public. Under the financial pressure of the Depression, artists were forced to engage in the debate about these artistic styles.

The most popular painters of the 1930s were the regionalists, who produced nostalgic scenes of traditional American life. Importantly, the regionalists were interested in painting scenes from particular local areas of the United States. They saw the tendency toward a national, or even international, style in art as damaging to local traditions and values. Painter Thomas Hart Benton (1889–1975) won many admirers when he said he would rid America of the "dirt" of European influence. Led by Benton, the regionalists argued that European modernism was obscure and elitist. Art, they believed, should be understandable by all. Grant Wood's (1891–1942) haunting *American Gothic* (1930) is a classic of regionalist painting. Showing a stern couple standing guard over their farmstead, *American Gothic* links the couple's moral values and beliefs with their sense of place. Regionalist painters like Benton were conservative in their work and their politics. However, other painters used realistic scenes to take a more radical approach. The social realists used their art to expose the suffering of people on farms and in factories during the Depression. They hoped their art would have a positive political effect, and they worked with the Works Progress Administration (WPA) to produce "public art for the public good." Members of this group include Ben Shahn (1898–1969), Reginald Marsh (1898–1954), and Philip Evergood (1901–1973).

Although there was a strong demand in the art world for art that was distinctively American in its subject matter, Europeans did start to influence American art. The worsening economic and political situation in Europe brought many artists, and their abstract styles of painting, to the United States. By the end of the decade, modernist and abstract art was beginning to find an audience in this country, and they became more popular in the following decades.

Some painters mixed the two approaches. Edward Hopper's (1882–1967) work falls somewhere between realism and abstraction. Although he is some-

Grant Wood's oil painting
American Gothic.
*Reproduced by permission of the
Visual Artists and Galleries
Association, Inc. for Grant Wood.*

times described as a "scene" painter, Hopper's near-deserted realistic urban landscapes have an abstract feel to them. In a Hopper painting, reality itself is strange and "unreal." Because he bridges the gap between realism and a modernist view of life as alienating and lonely, Hopper is among the most important artists of the decade. He has become known as the "Painter of Loneliness."

❖ FEDERAL SUPPORT FOR ARTS

The Federal Arts Project (FAP) tried to encourage all kinds of art and sculpture. It wanted to preserve American traditions, but it also wanted to

gangster movies and stories at the time. Although gangster movies tended to tell their stories from the gangster's point of view, even if they were usually also shown to be bad people, *Dick Tracy* offered the detective's point of view. In a clever sales gimmick, Quaker Oats sponsored a *Dick Tracy* radio show. By sending in cereal box tops, children could join Dick Tracy's Secret Service Patrol. Kids moved up through the ranks as their box top collection grew.

The Superman series began in 1939, published by *Action Comics*. Other action superheroes appeared over the following decade, but Superman remained the perfect American hero. An immigrant (from the planet Krypton), Superman was an ordinary man capable of amazing feats of strength, endurance, and even flying. He became a symbol of American values and power as World War II began.

The first of the Whitman Company's Big Little Books appeared in 1932. They were four hundred-page books alternating text and pictures on facing pages. Selling for ten cents, they adapted stories and characters from the comic strips. Flash Gordon, Dick Tracy, and Little Orphan Annie all appeared in Big Little Books. The first comic book was a collection of strips called *Funnies on Parade* (1933), given away free with Proctor and Gamble products. Published until the 1970s, the books were the most popular with school-age children during the 1930s and 1940s.

❖ WRITING AND SOCIAL CHANGE: TOUGH GUYS, WORKERS, AND SOUTHERNERS

American writers responded to the Depression in several ways. Some thought writing could bring about social change. Literary journalists documented the suffering of American people, modernists tried to understand the American self, and "tough-guy" writers offered a bleak view of the country in crisis. But what all these writers had in common was an urge to describe the American experience, and to make fiction relevant to the modern world.

Spurred by a sense that something was wrong, many writers went on the road in the 1930s. Sherwood Anderson's *Puzzled America* (1935), Theodore Dreiser's *Tragic America* (1931), and John Dos Passos's *In All Countries* (1934) are all based on the desperate stories these writers heard while traveling. Writers also challenged old ideas of literary value by trying to describe the "unexceptional American." What they came up with was an America that included homeless people, immigrants, and ethnic groups. These people had always been there, of course. But now for the first time fiction writers made them central characters in the American novel. This new focus on outsiders, misfits, and the misunderstood became a distinctive feature of American literature throughout the rest of the twentieth century.

Because they are about the lives of working people, also known as the "proletariat," such novels became known as "proletarian novels." Among others, Nelson Algren's *Somebody in Boots* (1935), Henry Roth's *Call It Sleep* (1935), and Richard Wright's *Uncle Tom's Children* (1938) are all important because they discuss everyday experiences. In his *U.S.A.* trilogy (1938), Dos Passos deepened the description of "ordinary" America by using newsreel scripts, short biographies, and advertising pitches to recreate the feel of American life. Other writers became linked with particular places or events, especially for the way they describe their "ordinariness." A group of "California" novelists included Nathanael West (1903–1940) and Dashiell Hammett (1894–1961), while William Faulkner (1897–1962) was linked with the rural South. Other radical writers, such as Mary Heaton Vorse (1874–1966), wrote about strikes and labor struggles.

Most writers of the time embraced modern life and hoped to use their skills to improve the economic and social situation. The conservative Agrarian Movement hoped to recreate a rural and distinctively "Southern" way of life to balance the modern "American" way. In 1930, poets John Crowe Ransom, Donald Davidson, Allen Tate, and Robert Penn Warren along with eight others wrote *I'll Take My Stand,* a pamphlet attacking modern values. The book became known as the "Southern Manifesto," and was listed as being by "Twelve Southerners," since that was the number of people in the group. The twelve had a similar approach to that of the regionalist painters, in that they believed modern life was responsible for poverty, crime, and social disorder. They favored a return to "traditional" moral values, based on local needs and traditions. The Agrarian Movement more or less ignored the racism, poverty, and injustice that still gripped much of the South.

Popular fiction also focused on American life in the 1930s. Writers such as Hammett, James M. Cain, Horace McCoy, and Raymond Chandler first worked on pulp magazines such as *Black Mask* and *Dime Detective.* From those early short stories they developed the hard-boiled detective novel into one of the most popular and enduring types of fiction from the 1930s and 1940s. Usually written from the point of view of the cynical main character, hard-boiled novels often involve crime, corruption, and violence. Their bleak take on the world is similar to the proletarian novel, but hard-boiled fiction tends not to be openly political or to offer solutions. Instead the tough main character finds that the best way of dealing with modern life is to confront it with courage, honesty, and a loaded gun. The best tough-guy novels of the period include Hammett's *The Maltese Falcon* (1930), Cain's *The Postman Always Rings Twice* (1934), McCoy's *They Shoot Horses, Don't They?* (1935), and Chandler's *The Big Sleep* (1939).

❖ HOLLYWOOD'S GOLDEN AGE

The Depression era is thought to be the most important in the history of film. This golden age of Hollywood was fed by technological advances and, surprisingly, large amounts of money. While many independent studios closed down in the 1930s, the major studios looked like a safe bet for nervous investors. It was also a period when talented writers, directors, and technicians migrated to Hollywood from New York and overseas. But while Hollywood flourished in some ways, in others it was unchanged. As the eye-rolling slaves in the box-office smash *Gone With the Wind* (1939) demonstrate, African American roles in the movies were very limited. Hollywood also came under fire for showing sexual images on screen. In July 1934, the Production Code laid down rules about what could and could not be shown in movies. Former postmaster general Will H. Hays (1879–1954) was hired to administer the code. The "Hays Office" regulated everything, from the hemlines of dresses to making sure the bad guys were always punished.

In what was known as the "studio system," each movie studio developed its own style. Warner Brothers made socially conscious movies, such as *Heroes for Sale* (1932) and the anti-lynching movie *They Won't Forget* (1937). Paramount was known for stylish, witty projects, such as Cecil B. DeMille's *Cleopatra* (1934) and Ernst Lubitsh's *Angel* (1937), starring Marlene Dietrich. Metro-Goldwyn-Mayer (M-G-M) specialized in screwball comedies and light thrillers, such as the *Thin Man* series. Universal made horror movies, including James Whale's famous *Frankenstein* (1931), with Boris Karloff (1887–1969) in the lead role. Under the studio system, studios made and distributed films to their own chains of theaters. Groups of actors, directors, and others were made employees and had little choice in the projects they worked on. Studios divided their features into "A" and "B" movies. The A-movies were big-budget, star-studded features, but the "cheapie" B-movies were cranked out at a rate of one a week and ran alongside the main feature. Very occasionally a B-movie would be a hit, but they were often used for stylistic experiment or were aimed at smaller audiences.

Duck Soup, *starring the Marx Brothers, is considered one of the funniest American films of the twentieth century.* **Reproduced by permission of the Kobal Collection.**

Academy of Motion Picture Arts and Science Awards (The Oscars)

1930 Production: *All Quiet on the Western Front* **(Universal)**
Actor: George Arliss in *Disraeli*
Actress: Norma Shearer in *The Divorcee*
Direction: Louis Milestone for *All Quiet on the Western Front*

1931 Production: *Cimarron* **(RKO)**
Actor: Lionel Barrymore in *A Free Soul*
Actress: Marie Dressler in *Min and Bill*
Direction: Norman Taurog for *Skippy*

1932 Production: *Grand Hotel* **(M-G-M)**
Actor: Frederic March in *Dr. Jekyll and Mr. Hyde* and Wallace Beery in *The Champ*
Actress: Helen Hayes in *The Sin of Madelon Claudet*
Direction: Frank Borsage for *Bad Girl*

1933 Production: *Cavalcade* **(Fox)**
Actor: Charles Laughton in *The Private Life of Henry VIII*
Actress: Katharine Hepburn in *Morning Glory*
Direction: Frank Lloyd for *Cavalcade*

1934 Production: *It Happened One Night* **(Columbia)**
Actor: Clark Gable in *It Happened One Night*
Actress: Claudette Colbert in *It Happened One Night*
Direction: Frank Capra for *It Happened One Night*

Perhaps because Prohibition (the legal ban on the manufacture and sale of alcoholic beverages) made real-life gangsters into famous outlaws, the 1930s were the golden age of gangster movies. Warner Brothers made *Doorway to Hell* (1930), *Little Caesar* (1930), and *G-Men* (1935). James Cagney was the Warner Brothers' big star, but the other studios also had their stable of leading men. The 1930s gangster movie craze made stars of Humphrey Bogart, Edward G. Robinson, James Stewart, and Gary Cooper.

Hollywood in the 1930s was also famous for the "screwball" comedy. Known for their witty dialogue, films like *The Thin Man* (1934) pair strong female characters with their male equals. Another example is Frank Capra's *It Happened One Night* (1934), which matches Clark Gable (1901–1960) and Claudette Colbert (1903–1996). The Marx Brothers'

1935 Production: *Mutiny on the Bounty* **(M-G-M)**
Actor: Victor McLaglen in *The Informer*
Actress: Bette Davis in *Dangerous*
Direction: John Ford for *The Informer*

1936 Production: *The Great Ziegfeld* **(M-G-M)**
Actor: Paul Muni in *The Story of Louis Pasteur*
Actress: Luise Rainer in *The Great Ziegfeld*
Direction: Frank Capra for *Mr. Deeds Goes to Town*

1937 Production: *The Life of Emile Zola*
Actor: Spencer Tracy in *Captains Courageous*
Actress: Luise Rainer in *The Good Earth*
Supporting Actor: Joseph Schildkraut in *The Life of Emile Zola*
Direction: Leo McCarey for *The Awful Truth*

1938 Production: *You Can't Take It With You* **(Columbia)**
Actor: Spencer Tracy in *Boys' Town*
Actress: Bette Davis in *Jezebel*
Supporting Actress: Fay Bainter in *Jezebel*
Direction: Frank Capra for *You Can't Take It With You*

1939 Production: *Gone With the Wind* **(Selznick-M-G-M)**
Actor: Robert Donat in *Goodbye, Mr. Chips*
Actress: Vivien Leigh in *Gone With the Wind*
Supporting Actor: Thomas Mitchell in *Stagecoach*
Supporting Actress: Hattie McDaniel in *Gone With the Wind*

series of films were in a comedy class of their own. With their sharp dialogue and madcap stunts, movies such as *Duck Soup* (1933) and *A Night at the Opera* (1935) are among the best comic films ever made.

Audiences in the 1930s also delighted in animated films. Mickey Mouse had first appeared in 1928 and remained a firm favorite throughout the 1930s. Disney won a special Oscar in 1932 for a Mickey cartoon featuring Donald Duck. Warner Brothers' character Popeye the Sailor was Disney's main competitor. But short movies such as "The Three Little Pigs" (1933) kept Disney ahead. One of the "Silly Symphonies" shorts, called *Flowers and Trees* (1933), was the first film made in full Technicolor. Disney set a new standard for animated movies in 1937 with the feature-length *Snow White and the Seven Dwarfs*.

In the depths of the Depression, the lavish musicals of choreographer Busby Berkeley (1895–1976) at M-G-M offered spectacular entertainment based on dance numbers. *Gold Diggers of 1933* (1933), *Stars Over Broadway* (1934), and *Stage Struck* (1936) are all presented like stage shows. The cinematic view of dancers taken from above, known as the "Berkeley top shot," is a hallmark of these films. The ten movies made by Fred Astaire (1899–1987) and Ginger Rogers (1911–1995) were more elegant and graceful. *Top Hat* (1935), *Shall We Dance?* (1937), and the rest are distinctly more refined in comparison with the Berkeley extravaganzas.

❖ MUSIC IN THE 1930s

Throughout the 1930s, various American musical styles were invented or recorded in the United States. From wandering bluesmen to classical composers, archivists, and radio producers, there was a drive to record American music for the future. Many producers went in search of new, "unspoiled" talent. They recorded their discoveries on wax cylinders, the latest in recording technology. Sponsored by colleges and federal programs, such collections helped turn folk music from the South into a national art form. The jukebox and the home phonograph helped spread traditional music around the country. But most important of all was the radio. The Depression boosted radio listenership at the same time as it dented record sales and audiences for live concerts. In 1935 the Metropolitan Opera Company made the first of its popular broadcasts from New York City, while Nashville radio station WSM's "Grand Ole Opry" programs helped bring hillbilly music to a national audience. After Prohibition ended in 1933, the new bars and taverns bought jukeboxes to attract customers. Within five years there were around 250,000 "juke joints" nationwide.

The Carter Family was the most important hillbilly act of the decade. Based on a traditional brand of Southeastern guitar-based folk music, the Carters' style was a major influence on musicians who followed. A more popular brand of hillbilly music was represented by "Singing Brakeman" Jimmie Rodgers (1897–1933). Rodgers was famous for his distinctive "blue yodel" sound and became known as the "father of country music." "Singing Cowboys," such as Roy Rogers (1911–1998) and Gene Autry (1907–1998), sang sentimental songs about the days of the frontier. "Western music," as it became known, came to include almost all of what was categorized by the twenty-first century as "Country." Beyond the mainstream, folklorist Robert W. Gordon (1888–1961) used more than a thousand recording cylinders to create the Archive of American Folk Song. Sponsored by the Federal Music Project (FMP) and several universities, the archive made southern folk music popular with north-

Busby Berkeley was a revolutionary filmmaker and choreographer. He created many musical extravaganzas onscreen including 1933's 42nd Street. *Reproduced by permission of the Corbis Corporation.*

ern intellectuals. The most important folk singer of the period was Huddie "Leadbelly" Ledbetter (1885–1949), who was "discovered" in jail in Louisiana. In 1934 Leadbelly became the darling of the northern academic elite when he debuted at the Modern Languages Association conference in Philadelphia.

Because they were cheaper than hiring a whole band, lone bluesmen such as Robert Johnson (1911–1938) and Blind Lemon Jefferson (1897–1929) were popular in the Depression. Many black bluesmen migrated to Chicago to escape segregation and racism in the South. Although "the blues" came from the rural South, by the end of the decade the blues had become urban music. Jazz in the 1930s gradually became an interracial music, played by big bands and marketed as "new jazz" or swing. Count Basie (1904–1984), Lester Young (1909–1959), and others began to turn jazz into what would eventually become "bop" in the 1940s. Band leaders such as Benny Goodman, Tommy Dorsey, Artie Shaw, and Glenn Miller made jazz respectable to the white middle classes. Gospel music was the church-going cousin of the blues and jazz. As the Depression turned churches into social centers, Thomas (not Tommy) Dorsey (1899–1993) brought in music. Gospel entered its golden age in the 1940s. But its first superstar, Mahalia Jackson (1911–1972), made her first recording in 1937.

American classical composers such as Aaron Copland, Virgil Thomson, Elliott Carter, Marc Blitzstein, and David Diamond trained with Nadia Boulanger in Paris in the 1920s. Copland in particular searched for an American style, and wrote a book, *What to Listen for in Music* (1938), to make classical music more popular. Other composers who matured in the 1930s include Roy Harris (*First Symphony,* 1933) and Samuel Barber (*Adagio for Strings,* 1936). George Gershwin, one of the most famous of all American composers, produced *Of Thee I Sing* and the opera *Porgy and Bess* in 1935. Toward the end of the decade, European modernist composers came to the United States. Arnold Schoenberg, Paul Hindemith, Kurt Weill, Béla Bartók, Igor Stravinsky, and others would influence American music for years to come. Many of the immigrants earned their living writing film scores for Hollywood.

❖ THE FLOWERING OF AMERICAN THEATER

As in the other arts, drama and dance in the 1930s were experimental, engaged with social problems such as unemployment, and focused on American themes. Probably the most influential theater company was the Group Theatre, founded by Harold Clurman, Cheryl Crawford, and Lee Strasburg in 1931. Strasburg promoted method acting, through which an actor tries to "become" a character, adopting his or her hair style and other traits even when off-stage. Method acting later became the standard technique for American actors and it remained popular into the twenty-first century. Notable actors such as Morris Carnovsky, John Garfield, Elia Kazan, Lee J. Cobb, and J. Edgar Bromberg all performed in the Group Theatre's gritty and political productions. They had several Broadway hits, including Clifford Odets's (1906–1963) story of a New York City cab drivers' strike, *Waiting for Lefty* (1934). Just three nights in the writing, the play made theater history when the audience made itself part of the drama and began chanting "Strike! Strike!" as it ended.

The Federal Theatre Project (FTP) was established in 1935 to create a theater that was accessible to all. Headed by Hallie Flanagan, the FTP produced farces (comic drama), marionette shows, children's plays, and modern dramas in cities and towns across the United States. Sinclair Lewis and John C. Moffitt's *It Can't Happen Here* opened in 1935 in eighteen cities at the same time. Spin-offs such as the Negro Theatre Project, run by John Houseman (1902–1988) and Orson Welles (1915–1985), provided training for black theater artists. *The Swing Mikado,* a black version of Gilbert and Sullivan's operetta, was seen by 250,000 people in Chicago alone. Living Newspapers were the most acclaimed of the federal projects. They dramatized and interpreted current events, blending fact and fiction to inform and educate the audience. But conservative congressmen saw the FTP as a hotbed of left wing rebellion, and the FTP lost its funding in 1939.

Houseman and Welles founded the Mercury Theatre to present Marc Blitzstein's (1905–1964) pro-union political opera *The Cradle Will Rock* in 1937. The play began as an FTP production but had its funding withdrawn. Houseman and Welles went ahead anyway and later used the Mercury Theatre to produce several other plays, including a popular version of *Julius Caesar* in modern dress. The last production was Richard Wright and Paul Green's *Native Son* (1940). But the most notorious of the Mercury Theatre's projects was its radio version of H. G. Wells's *The War of the Worlds* (1938). Directed by the 24-year-old Welles, *The War of the Worlds* was broadcast on CBS radio on October 30. Because the play was presented as a news broadcast, thousands of listeners believed Martians had actually invaded. Panic spread as people called police stations and jumped in their cars to escape. In New York, sailors on shore leave were ordered back to their ships. Despite the fact that the broadcast was announced as a drama, it was so convincing that CBS had to promise not to air any more fictional news events.

Theater incomes fell throughout the 1930s as radio gained ground. But on Broadway the comedies of Moss Kaufman (1904–1961) and George S. Hart (1889–1961) and musicals like *Hellzapoppin'* (1938) managed to find success. The drama *Life With Father* (1939) ran for eight years. Depression themes were also popular, but perhaps the most surprising hit of the time was *Pins and Needles* (1937), a show about life in a textiles factory. Put on by the International Ladies Garment Workers Union, the comic revue ran for 1,100 performances. The performers had to take time off from their regular work to be in the show.

❖ DANCE AND OPERA

Martha Graham, Helen Tamiris, Doris Humphrey, and Charles Weldman founded the Dance Repertory Theatre in 1930. Their aim was to create an American style of dance to express the nation's energy and drive. Modern dance, as it was called, dealt with themes of American life. Dance Repertory Theatre productions used a bare stage and plain costumes to force audiences to concentrate on the dance itself. They also borrowed from American legends and literary classics. Graham's (1894–1991) most famous piece, *American Document* (1938), even draws on the Preamble to the Declaration of Independence. Tamiris (1905–1966) headed the Federal Theatre Project's New York-based Dance Project, and her work had a strong political edge. Her most famous piece is the pro-civil rights *How Long Brethren* (1937), but Tamiris was also influential in making dance central to the Broadway musical. A more popular kind of dance theater was produced by the American Ballet Company, founded by Lincoln Kirstein (1907–1996) in 1934, and the American Ballet Caravan. Both companies specialized in dances set to American popular music, such as ragtime and swing.

The big opera houses in New York and Chicago were hit hard by the stock market crash. But with help from the WPA and radio appeals for funds, New York's Metropolitan Opera Company managed to survive. American opera was a rare but consistent feature on the Met's stage. Joseph Deems Taylor's *Peter Ibbetson* premiered in 1931, while Virgil Thomson's *Four Saints in Three Acts* (with a libretto, or script, by Gertrude Stein) spent six weeks in New York in 1934. The most famous American opera of all is George Gershwin's *Porgy and Bess* (1935). Set in the black slum Catfish Row, *Porgy and Bess* tells the story of Porgy's love for Bess and his murder of her lover, Crown. It premiered in Boston to mixed critical response, before moving to New York. Gershwin's opera was the first major American operatic work to gain international recognition.

 For More Information

BOOKS

Allen, Frederick Lewis. *Since Yesterday: The 1930s in America, September 3, 1929–September 3, 1939*. New York: HarperCollins, 1986.

Beaumont, Newhall. *The History of Photography*. Boston: Little, Brown, 1982.

Blackman, Cally. *The 20s and 30s: Flappers and Vamps*. Milwaukee, WI: Gareth Stevens, 2000.

Cowley, Malcolm. *Think Back on Us—A Contemporary Chronicle of the 1930s*. Southern Illinois University Press, 1967.

Feinstein, Stephen. *The 1930s: From the Great Depression to the Wizard of Oz (Decades of the Twentieth Century)*. New York: Enslow Publishers, 2001.

Goulart, Ron. *Comic Book Culture: An Illustrated History.* Portland, OR: Collector's Press, 2000.

Gruber, J. Richard. *Thomas Hart Benton and the American South.* Augusta, GA: Morris Museum of Art, 1998.

Guthrie, Woody. *Bound for Glory.* New York: New American Library, 1995.

Manchel, Frank. *The Talking Clowns: From Laurel and Hardy to the Marx Brothers.* New York: Watts, 1976.

Mank, Gregory William. *Women in Horror Films, 1930s.* Jefferson, NC: McFarland and Company, 1999.

Mazo, Joseph H. *Prime Movers: The Makers of Modern Dance in America.* New York: Morrow Quill Paperbacks, 1980.

Oermann, Robert K. *A Century of Country: An Illustrated History of Country Music.* New York: TV Books, 1999.

Park, Marlene. *New Deal for Art: The Government Art Projects of the 1930s With Examples from New York City and State.* New York: Gallery Association of New York State, 1977.

Press, Petra. *The 1930s (Cultural History of the United States Through the Decades).* San Diego: Lucent, 1999.

Schatz, Thomas. *The Genius of the System: Hollywood Filmmaking in the Studio Era.* New York: Pantheon, 1988.

Shaw, Arnold. *Let's Dance: Popular Music in the 1930s.* New York: Oxford University Press, 1998.

Smith, Wendy. *Real Life Drama: The Group Theatre and America 1931–1940.* New York: Knopf, 1990.

Southern, Eileen. *The Music of Black Americans: A History.* New York: Norton, 1983.

Strubel, John Warthen. *The History of American Classical Music.* New York: Facts on File, 1995.

Swortzell, Lowell. *Six Plays for Young People from the Federal Theatre Project (1936–1939).* New York: Greenwood Press, 1986.

Weisberger, Bernard, A., ed. *The WPA Guide to America: The Best of 1930s America as Seen by the Federal Writers Project.* New York: Pantheon, 1985.

Wilson, Charles Reagan, and William Ferris, eds. *Encyclopedia of Southern Culture.* Chapel Hill: University of North Carolina Press, 1989.

Wollstein, Hans J. *Vixens, Floozies and Molls: 28 Actresses of Late 1920s and 1930s Hollywood.* New York: McFarland, 1999.

WEB SITES

Dirks, Tim. "Greatest Films of the 1930s." Greatest Films. http://www.filmsite. org/30sintro.html (accessed July 23, 2002).

"Great Depression and World War II, 1929–1945: Art and Entertainment in the 1930s and 1940s." Library of Congress: American Memory Timeline. http://

memory.loc.gov/ammem/ndlpedu/features/timeline/depwwii/art/art.html (accessed July 23, 2002).

Business and the Economy

Chronology

1930: McGraw-Electric of Elgin, Illinois, introduces the first electric toaster.

1930: **March 6** Birds Eye Frozen Foods go on sale in Springfield, Massachusetts.

1930: **June 17** Against the advice of his advisers, President Herbert Hoover signs the Smoot-Hawley Tariff—the highest tax on trade in American history—into law. In response, other countries introduce similar trade barriers, further damaging U.S. exports.

1930: **December 11** New York's Bank of the United States goes out of business. Four hundred thousand depositors lose their savings.

1931: **May 4** The coal miners' strike in Harlan County, Kentucky, turns into a gunfight. Three guards and one miner are killed. Many more are wounded.

1931: **August 4** Martial law is declared in Oklahoma, as Governor William H. Murray attempts to shut down oil fields to raise prices. Soon after, in Texas, Governor Ross Sterling does the same.

1932: **January 22** Congress authorizes the Reconstruction Finance Corporation (RFC) to help struggling businesses.

1932: **March 7** Police fire on demonstrators at Ford's plant at Dearborn, Michigan. Four are killed and more than one hundred are injured.

1932: **July 7** The Dow Jones Industrial Average hits an all-time low of 41.22.

1933: **March 6** To stop the banking crisis, President Franklin D. Roosevelt declares a national bank holiday.

1933: **May 12** Congress passes the Federal Emergency Relief Act, awarding the states $500 million in aid.

1933: **June 16** The Glass-Steagall Act provides for government regulation of banking. Congress also approves the National Industrial Recovery Act and the Farm Credit Act.

1933: **November 9** The Civil Works Administration begins providing emergency jobs for four million unemployed.

1934: During the month of May, 300 million tons of topsoil are blown from the Plains states as far as the Atlantic Ocean.

1934: **January 31** The Farm Mortgage Refinancing Act protects farmers from creditors.

1934: **June 6** The Securities and Exchange Commission (SEC) is set up to oversee financial markets.

1934: **July 16** A general strike begins in San Francisco, led by the International Longshoremen's Association. It lasts for eleven days.

1935: **February 16** The Connally Hot Oil Act regulates the production of oil to support prices.

1935: **June 26** The National Youth Administration is set up to provide jobs for
young people.

1935: **August 14** The Social Security Act creates a nationwide system of old age
pensions and unemployment benefits.

1935: **November 9** The Committee for
Industrial Organizations (CIO) splits
off from the American Federation of
Labor (AFL).

1936: **February 14** United Rubber Workers
stage the first ever sit-down strike
when they refuse to leave the
Goodyear Tire and Rubber Plant No. 2.

1936: **June 29** Congress passes the Merchant Marine Act, subsidizing the
American cargo fleet.

1936: **December 31** A sit-down strike begins
at the General Motors' Chevrolet body
plant in Flint, Michigan. It lasts until
the following February.

1937: In the course of the year, American
industry is affected by 4,740 work
stoppages, strikes, and lockouts.

1937: **February 11** The sit-down strike at
General Motors' Flint, Michigan, plant
is ended when the company agrees to
recognize the United Automobile
Workers (UAW) as sole bargaining
agent for workers.

1937: **March 2** United States Steel avoids a
strike by allowing its workers to form
unions.

1937: **March 29** In the legal case *West
Coast Hotel v. Parrish* the Supreme
Court upholds the minimum wage for
women.

1937: **May 30** Chicago police open fire on a
union picnic of Republic Steel workers. Ten are killed and eighty-four are
injured. The event is known as the
"Memorial Day Massacre."

1938: **June 15** The Fair Labor Standards Act
limits the working week to forty-four
hours. After that, overtime pay is due
to workers. A minimum wage is set at
25 cents per hour. 12.5 million Americans are affected by these changes.

1938: **June 21** Congress passes the Emergency Relief Appropriations Act,
which continues government assistance to the unemployed.

1938: **June 27** President Roosevelt signs
the U.S. Food, Drug, and Cosmetic
Act. It updates the 1906 Pure Food
and Drug Act, taking technological
advances such as canned and frozen
food into account.

1939: The General Electric Company introduces fluorescent lighting.

1939: The electronic instrument firm
Hewlett-Packard is founded.

1939: **June 26** Pan-American Airways
begins the first transatlantic passenger air service. The flight takes more
than four hours.

Overview

The 1930s were a turning point for the economy of the United States. In the nineteenth century, the economy had been driven by heavy industry and by the expanding frontier. As the nation grew, it demanded more goods. From railway lines to locomotives, ships, and building materials, American industry was working at full tilt. World War I helped continue the trend, but by the end of the 1920s things had changed. The American economy no longer demanded enough goods to keep heavy industry in business on such a large scale. By 1931, most of the railroads had been built, and even the automobile industry was struggling. With less money to spend, people kept their cars longer, put them in storage, or simply went without. Agricultural products, oil, and coal flooded the market and prices fell. The old economy had almost stopped working.

For a while it was feared that low prices, high unemployment, and over-supply would never go away. "Stagnationist" economists thought that the economy had literally stagnated (completely stopped developing) and that it would never again be as dynamic as it was in the past. Fortunately, they were wrong. The 1930s saw the birth of a new kind of capitalism, based on service industries such as medical care and entertainment, and on consumer products like radios, televisions, refrigerators, and washing machines. These new industries created what became known as a consumer economy, an economy based on the manufacture of goods and services that are purchased and used directly by individuals for consumption. But the consumer economy was in its infancy in the 1930s, and most people were too poor to enjoy it.

One area where the new economy took off quickly was groceries. The first supermarket opened in 1930, and by 1939 there were more than five thousand supermarkets across the country. Canned and frozen food became popular, and consumers began to worry about the safety of processed food. Meanwhile the chemical and oil industries produced new fuels needed for the growing aviation industry and new materials such as rayon and nylon. These materials led to new products and markets. In the late 1930s the economy began to respond better to what people wanted, and economic hardships began to ease. Government policy helped as well. President Franklin D. Roosevelt's economic plan, the New Deal helped the construction industry by funding new public buildings. By improving access to electricity around the country, the New Deal also created a market for electrical goods.

The new economy led to major changes in the workplace. Historically, the United States has suffered some of the bitterest industrial disputes in the developed world. In the 1930s, workers at Ford's River Rouge plant in Michigan were paid extra to spy on their coworkers. In Chicago, Minneapolis, San Francisco, and elsewhere, protesters were injured and killed by hired thugs. During the Allegheny coal strike of 1934, strikers' homes were bombed. Six union organizers lost their lives. Between 1933 and 1936, the Pinkerton Detective Agency earned around $1.7 million from policing factories and mines.

With the Wagner Act of 1935, the Roosevelt administration gave labor unions a bigger say in working conditions and pay. Many industrialists were angry. But for "consumer" industries such as real estate, banking, insurance, furniture, and household goods, higher wages meant more profits because people would have more money to spend. The New Deal brought union organizers, politicians, and consumer industrialists together. These groups wanted more protection for workers from market forces, they wanted the financial markets to be better organized, and they wanted wealth to be shared more fairly through taxation. These ideas held sway into the next decade as the United States entered World War II (1938–45) and helped prepare the economy for the consumer spending boom that followed.

David Dubinsky (1892–1982) Born David Dobnievski in Russian Poland, Dubinsky spent eighteen months in a Polish prison for being a labor agitator. When he was nineteen, he escaped to New York, where he became a master of the cloak-cutting craft. He rose to the office of president of the International Ladies Garment Workers Union (ILGWU) in 1932. By 1934 the ILGWU was the third largest labor union in the United States, with 200,000 members. Dubinsky was a prominent pro-Roosevelt campaigner. He organized several successful strikes during the 1930s and finally retired from the post in 1966. *Photo courtesy of the Library of Congress.*

Armand Hammer (1898–1990) A physician, pharmacist, mine operator, grain merchant, distiller, and many other things besides, Armand Hammer was a millionaire for seven of his nine decades. Although he was one of the most prominent tycoons of the 1930s, his businesses were not always strictly legal. During Prohibition, Hammer's pharmacy's best-selling product was a solution of ginger that was 85 percent alcohol, and in 1976 Hammer was convicted of making illegal contributions to Richard Nixon's 1972 presidential campaign. Nevertheless, Hammer remained an active and influential man in political circles. *Photo reproduced by permission of Archive Photos, Inc.*

Howard Hughes (1905–1975) Howard Hughes was an engineering and movie tycoon who made his name as a pioneering aviator. When hired stunt pilots refused to risk death for his movie *Hell's Angels* (1930), Hughes did the flying himself. On August 13, 1935, he broke the speed record in his H-1 racing airplane, achieving 352.388 miles per hour. In 1938, he flew around the world in a record-breaking three days, nineteen hours, and eight minutes. Despite his reputation for adventure and excitement, Hughes's private life was unhappy. As he aged, he became a drug addict and a recluse. *Photo courtesy of the Library of Congress.*

Haroldson Lafayette Hunt Jr. (1889–1974) As a child, oil tycoon Haroldson Lafayette Hunt Jr. was talented at mathematics and card games. By age sixteen, he was competing at cards with experienced adults, and soon became a professional gambler. In the 1920s, knowing nothing about geology, Hunt made several lucky oil strikes. Throughout the 1930s, he made deals with governments around the world to protect oil interests, and by 1942 he was the richest man in the United States. Hunt was also a bigamist: he had married two women and supported these two families, as well as a mistress and his child with her. When he died, his will was contested by all three families, none of whom had ever known about the others.

Samuel Insull (1859–1938) Electricity tycoon Samuel Insull was born and raised in England but became an American citizen in 1896. In 1912 he set up the Middle West Utilities Company, which took advantage of the spread of electricity in the 1920s. When Insull's companies collapsed, investors lost between two and three billion dollars. Although the energy industry as a whole suffered heavy losses, the press seemed to blame Insull personally for the crash and the Depression. Accused of buying political influence, he went on trial in 1934 and was acquitted of all charges. He lived the remainder of his life in Paris. *Photo reproduced by permission of Archive Photos, Inc.*

Howard Johnson (1885–1977) In 1924, Howard Johnson invested $300 in an ice cream recipe belonging to an elderly German immigrant. Four years later, his gross income from ice cream sales was $240,000. Howard Johnson food outlets were one of the great successes of the 1930s. Famous for his roadside restaurants, Johnson became known as the "Host of the Highways." The war hit Johnson's business hard, but he acquired contracts to supply food for workers in the munitions factories and managed to keep the company afloat. In the 1950s he branched out into motor lodges, and by 1956 the gross income of the Howard Johnson Company was $175,530,695.

John L. Lewis (1880–1969) John L. Lewis was the dominant figure of the 1930s labor movement. He became president of the United Mine Workers in 1909 and reached the height of his powers as president of the Congress of Industrial Organizations (CIO) between 1933 and 1937. In those years he worked closely with the federal government to improve the influence of labor unions. He cultivated the image of himself sharing sauerkraut and beer with President Roosevelt. The downturn of 1937 ended his period of influence, but by then his efforts had improved the lives of millions of industrial workers. *Photo courtesy of the Library of Congress.*

Rose Pesotta (1896–1965) Rose Pesotta helped David Dubinsky run the International Ladies Garment Workers Union (ILGWU). She was one of the most militant female labor activists, working as the only "woman organizer" at the United Auto Workers (UAW) strike in Flint, Michigan. Her great skill was in talking to female relatives of male strikers to win their support. During the Flint Campaign, she was beaten up by company thugs and left with a permanent hearing impairment. She was one of very few women to succeed in the male-dominated labor movement of the 1930s. *Photo courtesy of the Library of Congress.*

◆◆ *Topics in the News* • • • • • • • • • • • • • • • • •

❖ THE SLOW CREEP OF THE DEPRESSION

On October 24 and October 29 in 1929, around nine billion dollars were wiped off the New York Stock Exchange. The "Great Crash" put an end to the "roaring twenties" and began the financial slump that was known as the Great Depression. There had been other slumps in the past, but the effects had always been limited to particular industries or regions. This time the entire nation suffered. The new national media was partly to blame. By reporting events from around the country, the media made the slump seem worse than it really was in the early stages. People lost confidence in the economy, and it began to spiral out of control.

Unlike the crash, the Depression came on slowly. Politicians and business leaders claimed it would be no more than part of the normal business cycle. President Herbert Hoover (1874–1964) led the optimists, claiming in May 1930 that the worst was over. But to most people it was obvious that the situation was getting worse, even after the crash stock prices kept falling. General Motors (GM) stock fell from $212 per share in 1928 to just $8 in 1931. In 1932, American industry produced only half what it had made in 1929. Wages kept falling, with unskilled workers being paid only seven cents an hour. By 1932, most politicians and business leaders had given up on the idea that the economy would improve quickly or easily.

There were several reasons why the Great Depression was so severe. Some areas of the economy had been struggling since the 1920s. Farming was especially weak. By 1920, for the first time ever, more Americans lived in towns and cities than on farms. They made more money in factories than on farms. At the time, American farmers earned only 40 percent of the average wage for laborers in the cities. When the Depression hit, hundreds of thousands more gave up their land and moved to urban centers. Drought made the misery worse. In the West and Plains states, farmland dried up and literally blew away. Dust storms buried small buildings, and livestock starved. Whole communities of people packed up whatever they could carry with them and set off in search of work.

During the 1920s, American farmers had borrowed money and modernized their farms. They bought machinery, land, and used fertilizers to get as much from the soil as possible. Bumper crops around the world in the late 1920s made prices drop; with more food available, the prices growers could charge for their crops went down. Farmers entered the 1930s heavily in debt. By 1932, they were selling their crops for less than half what they were worth in 1929. In 1930, the Hoover administration

Unemployment and the Changing Workforce

Labor Force Unemployed (Percent)

1928	4.2
1932	23.6
1936	16.9
1940	14.6

Between 1930 and 1940, the number of working women rose from 10.7 million to 12.8 million. At the same time the total labor force grew from 48.8 million to 52.7 million. By 1940, women accounted for 24.3 percent of American workers.

Source: U.S. Department of Labor.

had implemented the Smoot-Hawley Tariff, a high tax designed to protect American farmers by reducing the quantity of imported goods, including food, coming into the country. It did not work as planned, however, and the economy continued to lose momentum. The troubled banks began to call in their loans, and many farmers were forced out of business.

Other industries suffered as well. In mining, wages fell around 12 percent in the 1920s. This meant that millions of Americans could not afford to buy the electrical and other goods that were coming on the market. As a result, there was an overproduction of consumer goods, oil, and food. These products had to be sold at a loss. The banks loaned money to people who wanted to buy cars and consumer goods. This hid the fact that consumers didn't have the money to pay for them. Once investors realized this was happening and stopped supporting such bad loans, the economy began to crumble.

Many attempts to fix the economy during the early 1930s in fact made it worse. Business leaders advised "belt-tightening" and cutbacks in spending. But since the problem was that nobody was spending money, spending even less money could not help. Some businesses attempted to ride out the storm by working together. But President Hoover stepped up antitrust prosecutions against those who tried to control the market in this way. It was a policy that made the problem of oversupply worse. With companies competing instead of cooperating, the market was flooded with consumer

"Hoovered"

When President Herbert Hoover (1874–1964) failed to save the country from the Depression, he became the target of bitter jokes. They included a series of "Hooverisms":

"Hooverville" was the name given to shanty towns where the homeless and many of the unemployed lived. During the Depression every major city had its Hooverville.

When gasoline became too expensive, many people began towing their automobiles with horses. Cars towed this way became known as "Hoovercarts."

One of the enduring images of the Depression is the beggar with his empty pants pockets turned out to show he has nothing. The turned out pants pockets became known as "Hooverflags."

goods and oil, and prices fell. Hoover also refused to pay farmers to produce less and avoided trade agreements that might have eased the problems of American industry. The election of Franklin D. Roosevelt (1882–1945) in 1932 marked the start of a more flexible, imaginative approach to solving the Depression. While his New Deal had many faults, its effect was to rescue the American economy from the worst downturn in history.

❖ A NEW PRESIDENT AND A NEW DEAL

Until October 24, 1929, the American economy was run by business for business. The free market was allowed to govern prices and production levels. Herbert Hoover (1874–1964), who served as secretary of commerce between 1921 and 1928, called it the "American System." The crash of 1929, in the first year of Hoover's presidency, exposed the weaknesses of the system. Yet even after the crash, Hoover insisted that the market would right itself. He stuck to his conservative view that business could save itself, and he tried to persuade business leaders to hold their nerve. Hoover's "hands off" approach failed. Unemployment rose, factories closed, there were strikes, violent protests, and homelessness. The American System had to change.

Where Hoover had stuck to the system and failed, President Franklin D. Roosevelt (1882–1945), who swept to victory in the 1932 election, was

Residents of Hooverville
were unemployed citizens
financially devastated by
the Great Depression.
*Reproduced by permission of
the Corbis Corporation.*

more flexible. He talked to economists and business leaders about different ways of solving the Depression. At the center of his so-called "Brains
Trust" were three professors from Columbia University. Raymond Moley,
Rexford Guy Tugwell, and Adolf A. Berle were assisted by a number of
other experts from business, industry, law, and politics. These experts
devised a plan to support and control business. This plan for the American
economy was called the New Deal.

Although many companies feared the New Deal, objecting to a regulated, organized form of capitalism, a number of powerful corporations
supported it. These corporations included banks such as Goldman Sachs

and the Bank of America, as well as IBM, American Tobacco, and Coca Cola. Their support of this dramatic plan to change America really did change the nation. While the Republican Party had, to this point, enjoyed years of business support, these corporations instead became important donors to the Democratic Party well into the 1960s. In addition, many of these banks and corporations were led by ethnic Americans. So not only did the New Deal revolutionize American capitalism, it also gave ethnic Americans a voice at the highest levels of government.

Roosevelt tried to solve the Depression by breaking it down into a series of smaller problems. This sometimes meant his administration was accused of not knowing what it was doing. But it meant the New Deal could be flexible and realistic. One example is the National Recovery Administration (NRA), whose first head was Hugh S. Johnson (1882–1942). The NRA allowed businesses to work together to control markets, rather than competing against one another. Working together in "cartels" meant that companies did not produce too much. This in turn kept prices up and profits healthy. Other agencies set up government-run industries to control the market and regulate supply and prices. The main problem with this system was that smaller companies couldn't compete. On May 27, 1935, the Supreme Court ruled the NRA unconstitutional.

A key idea behind the New Deal was that if people were paid more they would spend more on goods and services. Title 7(a) of the National Industrial Recovery Act (NIRA), passed in June 1933, allowed labor unions to work with employers to get the best wage deals for their members. This was known as collective bargaining. Social security and unemployment compensation helped the growing number of homeless people. The taxation system was changed so that those who earned the most paid the most. The dollar was deliberately devalued on the world money markets to make exports more competitive. With the Agricultural Adjustment Act of 1933, farmers were even paid to leave land unplanted and to raise fewer animals; it also guaranteed farmers a minimum price for their goods, providing a system of farm price support that continues in altered form into the twenty-first century. The average American was much better off under Roosevelt's reforms.

By 1937, the American economy was doing well. Unemployment had been reduced by 50 percent in five years to 7.7 million. Business investment stood at $11 billion, almost ten times what it was in 1933. On the down side, government debt had risen dramatically. Even so, the New Dealers were convinced that their plan had worked and began trying to balance the budget. They cut back on government work programs and reduced spending elsewhere. Almost immediately, the economy collapsed again.

Between 1930 and 1940 the number of farm workers fell from 10.3 million to 8.9 million. In the same period the total national income from farming fell from 12.6 million dollars to just over nine million dollars. In 1909, farmers had to grow two bushels of wheat to be able to buy a pair of shoes. By 1933, that number had risen to nine bushels.

Despite the troubles, Roosevelt was able to put the New Deal back on course. Although stability had not quite returned by the time World War II began, the $240 billion spent on the war effort turned out to be just what the American economy needed. And the economy had fully recovered by the late 1940s.

❖ WORKING IN AMERICA

For the American worker, the 1930s turned out to be the most troubled decade of the century. As more workers joined unions, they were better able to protest about unfair treatment by employers. Many found that the only way to make themselves heard was to walk off the job, but this carried considerable risk since unions had no official power to protect their members. In Harlan County, Kentucky, miners lived in company towns where all the buildings, shops, and even the churches were built and owned by the mine operators. Going on strike meant losing your home, your friends, and your family. Living conditions were terrible. Between 1929 and 1931, 231 children died of malnutrition in Harlan County. Then in 1931, the mine operators cut wages by 10 percent. The United Mine Workers (UMW) began to gather support, and by March 1931 the workers and the companies were in open conflict. At Evarts (one of the three noncompany towns in Harlan County where most of the union workers had moved), strikers and company deputies exchanged gunfire, and there were several deaths. After two days of chaos, the National Guard managed to restore order. Workers who refused to give up their union membership were forced to leave. The rest had no choice but to go back to work and accept the company's conditions. What occurred in Harlan County was one of the worst incidents of its kind, but it was not unique.

In the 1930s the automakers and their workers clashed. Company henchmen beat up workers and used teargas and live ammunition to control strikers and protesters. Many people were injured and some were killed. Between January 1934 and July 1936, General Motors spent almost $1 million on private detectives and security guards to spy on its workers. At Ford, under chief Harry Bennett, the "service department" spied on and intimidated workers at Michigan's River Rouge plant. The autoworkers' and miners' experiences illustrate the realities faced by the more than 1,500,000 workers who went on strike in 1934 alone.

By mid-decade unions had managed to win legal safeguards for themselves and the workers they represented. Rising unemployment and falling wages persuaded American workers to join unions in huge numbers to fight against poor working conditions. In its attempt to force companies to help restart the economy, the Roosevelt administration actually encouraged workers to form unions to negotiate with employers. In 1935, John L. Lewis (1880–1969) founded the Committee for Industrial Organizations (CIO), later known as the Congress of Industrial Organizations, as a breakaway from the American Federation of Labor (AFL). Unskilled, blue-collar workers were among the most at risk in the Depression. And the AFL had objected to Lewis's idea of bringing unskilled workers into the labor union movement. It was because of the CIO that most of American industry was unionized by 1939.

In 1935, the CIO was boosted by the Wagner Act, which protected unionized workers from unfair treatment. In return, Lewis campaigned for Roosevelt's reelection in 1936. He spoke at campaign rallies and encouraged workers to vote Democrat. Lewis would later claim that every steel town was behind Roosevelt as a result of his campaign. Although the CIO lost much of its influence when the economy slumped again in 1937, ultimately it was the CIO, not the AFL, which improved conditions for blue-collar workers and persuaded the automobile and steel industries to accept unions.

Another important piece of legislation eased the plight of workers. The National Labor Relations Act (NLRA), which made it illegal for companies to break up unions, was passed by the Roosevelt administration in 1935. The United Automobile Workers (UAW) was formed soon after. Even so, on May 26, 1937, union leaders Dick Frankensteen (1907–1977) and Walter Reuther (1907–1970) were beaten up on an overpass near the main gate at River Rouge. Ford's hired thugs also beat up photographers and a group of women who happened to be there. But by 1937, the workers were winning in their struggle for fair treatment and pay.

Although organized union strikes did get results in some cases, walkout strikes did pose an obvious drawback: once outside the factory gates, strikers

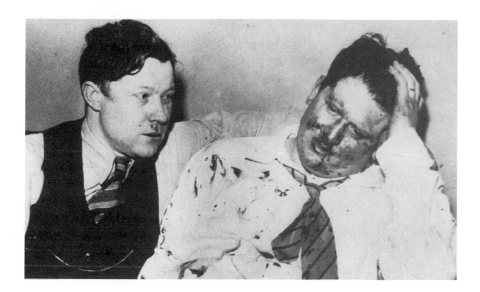

Union leaders like Richard T. Frankensteen and Walter Reuther often engaged in violent confrontations to achieve better benefits for their workers. **Reproduced by permission of the Corbis Corporation.**

might never be allowed back in. Unions quickly devised an alternative: the sit-down strike. The sit-down strike, where workers literally sat down on the job and refused to leave, was one of the most effective forms of protest in the 1930s. In 1936, the Bureau of Labor recorded forty-eight sit-downs, involving 88,000 workers. In 1937, there were 477 sit-downs, with 400,000 workers taking part. A sit-down strike at General Motors' Fisher auto body plant began on December 31, 1936, and lasted forty-four days. General Motors went to the courts to have its workers evicted, but the February 3 deadline came and went. Eventually, with Roosevelt himself encouraging talks, the protest ended on February 11, 1937. General Motors officially recognized the United Automobile Workers soon after, and before long many other large companies had accepted labor unions as part of pay bargaining talks.

❖ THE CHANGING AUTOMOBILE INDUSTRY

The automobile industry hardly existed as the twentieth century began. Yet by 1930 it had become the most important sector in the American economy. In 1929 a record five million vehicles were sold, and Americans spent one-tenth of their income buying and looking after their cars. When the economy collapsed, the auto industry was hit hard. By 1932, sales had dropped to just 1.33 million cars. Between 1929 and 1932, Ford Motor Company alone let over 80,000 of its workers go.

Ford, General Motors (GM), and Chrysler became known as the "Big Three" as their power in the car market increased. But although they gained market share in the 1930s, they didn't have an easy time. Ford soon lost its place as America's biggest carmaker as both GM and Chrysler made improvements to their models. In 1931, Chrysler's Plymouth and GM's Chevrolet were cheaper, better made, and more fuel-efficient than Ford's workmanlike Model A. Under the leadership of Alfred P. Sloan (1875–1966), GM's cars

were stylish and in tune with the age. Walter P. Chrysler (1875–1940) was also a brilliant and inspiring business leader. Henry Ford (1863–1947), in contrast, was old-fashioned and unwilling to accept change. By 1931, GM sold more than 43 percent of the cars in the United States to Ford's 28 percent. Two years later, Ford had fallen behind Chrysler into third place.

As the Depression deepened, the power of the Big Three increased. Independent automakers, such as Pierce-Arrow, Stutz, Marmon, Duesenberg, and Hupmobile, went out of business. (Independents sold one-quarter of all the cars on the road in 1925.) Of the luxury manufacturers, only Packard survived as an independent. It did so by building the smaller "junior" Packard in order to hang on to a shrinking market. By 1933, 95 percent of the market belonged to the Big Three.

❖ BANKING SYSTEM FAILURE

In the early twentieth century, Americans were split in their view of the banks. During the boom of the 1920s, many Americans saw bankers as careful, no-nonsense, trustworthy individuals. Yet among religious groups and in rural communities, investing and borrowing were often seen as a form of gambling. By the late 1920s, bankers such as J. P. Morgan (1867–1943) had great wealth, power, and influence, but government investigations in the 1930s showed the banks to have abused their powerful positions. For example, multimillionaire Morgan somehow managed to avoid paying tax between 1930 and 1931. By 1933 it seemed that nobody would trust the banks ever again.

During the 1920s, the banks loaned out far more money than they could possibly afford. This meant that when the stock market collapsed, banks had no assets to tide them over. When this began to happen, people rushed to take their savings out of the banks. Unfortunately, there was rarely enough cash available in any individual bank. Banks turned customers away, and many had to go out of business. In 1931 alone, 2,294 banks closed their doors permanently, taking their customers' money with them. In many cases people lost all the money they were saving for their retirement. Of course, the more times this happened, the more people panicked, and the more banks went under. By 1932, more than $9 million in savings had been wiped out.

By March 1933, the whole banking system of the United States was near collapse. On the night of his inauguration, President Roosevelt missed the celebration dinner to meet with bankers and government aides. Discussions went on over the weekend, and by Monday, March 6, a nationwide bank holiday was announced. By closing the banks for the next eight days, Roosevelt managed to calm the public mood. Public con-

OPPOSITE PAGE
Unions like the Teamsters fought for workers' rights and sometimes held strikes to achieve their goals. Here, Teamsters strike in Minnesota in 1934.

Farrell, Jacqueline. *The Great Depression*. San Diego, CA: Lucent Books, 1996.

Feinstein, Stephen. *The 1930s: from the Great Depression to the Wizard of Oz*. Berkeley Heights, NJ : Enslow Publishers, 2001.

Glassman, Bruce. *The Crash of '29 and the New Deal*. Morristown, NJ: Silver Burdett Co., 1986.

Holford, David M. *Herbert Hoover*. Springfield, NJ: Enslow, 1999.

Howe, Irving, and B.J. Widick. *The UAW and Walter Reuther*. New York: De Capo Books, 1973.

Joseph, Paul. *Herbert Hoover*. Minneapolis: Abdo & Daughters, 2001.

Larsen, Rebecca. *Franklin D. Roosevelt: Man of Destiny*. New York: F. Watts, 1991.

Lindop, Edmund. *Modern America: The Turbulent Thirties*. New York: F. Watts, 1970.

Meltzer, Milton. *Driven from the Land: The Story of the Dust Bowl*. New York: Benchmark Books, 2000.

Ross, Stewart. *Causes and Consequences of the Great Depression*. Austin, TX: Raintree Steck-Vaughn, 1998.

Schraff, Anne E. *The Great Depression and the New Deal: America's Economic Collapse and Recovery*. New York: F. Watts, 1990.

Sherrow, Victoria. *Hardship and Hope: America and the Great Depression*. New York: Twenty-First Century Books, 1997.

Stein, R. Conrad. *The Story of the Great Depression*. Chicago: Children's Press, 1985.

Steinbeck, John. *The Grapes of Wrath*. [1939]. New York: Penguin USA, 1992.

Stone, Lee Tanya. *The Great Depression and World War II*. Austin, TX: Raintree Steck-Vaughn, 2001.

Woog, Adam. *Roosevelt and the New Deal*. San Diego, CA: Lucent Books, 1998.

WEB SITES

America from the Great Depression to World War II: Photographs from the FSA-OWI, 1935–1945. http://memory.loc.gov/ammem/fsahtml/fahome.html (accessed July, 2002).

FDR Library and Digital Archives: K12 Learning Center. http://www.fdrlibrary.marist.edu/teach.html (accessed July, 2002).

Herbert Hoover Presidential Library. http://hoover.nara.gov/ (accessed July, 2002).

New Deal Network. http://newdeal.feri.org/ (accessed July, 2002).

chapter three *Education*

1930: Schools and colleges celebrate the two-thousandth anniversary of the birth of the Roman poet, Virgil.

1930: February 3 The first CBS *American School of the Air* broadcast is heard by more than 1.5 million schoolchildren.

1931: January The William H. Spencer High School opens in Columbus, Georgia. An all-black school, Spencer High becomes the model for "industrial schools," training students for jobs in factories.

1931: December President Herbert Hoover's National Advisory Committee on Education produces a report on American schools, finding them in good condition.

1932: The Educational Equality League is founded in Philadelphia. It aims to desegregate public schools, hire more black teachers, and put at least one African American on the Philadelphia school board.

1932: February 18 George S. Counts launches the "social reconstructionist" move-ment with his speech "Dare Progres-sive Education Be Progressive?"

1933: March 1 Philosopher John Dewey attacks the U.S. Chamber of Commerce for making cuts in education.

1933: April 17 The Civilian Conservation Corps (CCC) opens its first course. Although this New Deal agency is focused on environmental work, it also plays a key role in educating young people from poor back-grounds.

1933: April 24 Five thousand teachers march on Chicago city hall to demand ten months' back pay.

1933: December 14 A school bus is hit by a freight train in Crescent City, Florida. Ten children are killed and thirty are injured.

1934: The Progressive Education Associa-tion begins an eight-year study to prove that colleges need to be mod-ernized.

1934: Public schools buy one-third fewer textbooks than they did in 1930.

1934: Boycotts of segregated schools in Berwyn, Pennsylvania, lead to desegregation.

1934: **April 1** Twenty thousand schools, mainly in rural areas, have closed for lack of money.

1935: Nineteen states pass laws to make teachers swear loyalty oaths.

1935: **February 13** In Arkansas, an investigation into communism at Commonwealth College is authorized by the state's House of Representatives.

1935: **June 10** The Tennessee House of Representatives passes a statute to prevent the teaching of evolution.

1935: **June 26** The National Youth Administration (NYA) is set up to provide education and work for 16- to 25-year-olds.

1936: The U.S. Supreme Court hears the case of *Murray v. Maryland*. It rules that Maryland Law School should admit African American student Donald Murray or build a segregated law school. The law school admits Murray.

1937: **February 9** Senators Pat Harrison of Mississippi and Hugo Black of Alabama introduce a bill offering $100 million in federal aid to schools. The bill fails.

1937: **May 28** President Franklin D. Roosevelt repeals the infamous "red rider" to a Washington, D.C., appropriation bill. The rider had made teachers in the capital sign a loyalty oath.

1937: **November 21** Brookwood Labor College closes because of financial difficulties and internal disputes.

1938: The George-Deen Act is passed, appropriating $14.5 million for vocational education.

1938: **December 12** The U.S. Supreme Court orders the state of Missouri to provide equal education for African American law students.

1939: George S. Counts begins his campaign against communists in the American Federation of Teachers.

1939: Although 23.5 percent of college instructors are women, they make up only four percent of professors at state universities.

Overview

Education has always been at the heart of American democracy. The public school system was designed to take children from all backgrounds, all abilities, and give them the education they would need to find a job and better themselves. Before the 1930s, whole communities, from businesses to church leaders, felt proud of the schooling they provided for American youth. In many ways the public schools were a symbol of the promise of America.

During the Depression, the problems of American education rose to the surface. Although public education was free to all, the quality of schooling available in different parts of the country varied drastically. In some areas, such as the rural South, the public school system was starved for money. Many children in poor areas, especially African Americans, had very little experience of regular schooling. The Depression made the situation worse. Communities were unwilling and unable to spend as much on public schools as they had previously. As the economic situation further deteriorated, the public concentrated on other problems more than on public schooling. The National Economic League had named education the fourth most important national priority in 1930, but by 1932, it had dropped to thirty-second on the list.

As the Depression took hold, the financial support once offered to public schools by businesses was withdrawn. In the 1920s, businesses had eagerly supported the public school system. Money was loaned or donated for new buildings and books. Many construction firms saw building schools as an excellent business opportunity. Businesses also realized that public schools were training the clerks, typists, and book-keepers of the future. But when the Depression hit, struggling businesses removed their support. Public schools became dependent on lesser grants from the federal and state levels. With smaller budgets, schools closed and curriculum and teacher salaries were cut. In Chicago, the school board fired 1,400 teachers and cut salaries for the rest. Similar actions took place across the country. As school budgets dwindled, arguments erupted over the best methods of educating the nation's youth. These arguments changed American education for years to come.

Two of the greatest challenges to public education were quality of the curriculum and fairness. The promise of public education was that it would create knowledgeable citizens. But what knowledgeable citizens actually need to know has always been open for debate. For many in the 1930s, success in education meant going to college, and in theory this was possible for anyone with the ability. But in practice, college admission required knowledge of Latin or Greek, or being able to pass tests in algebra. These subjects were rarely taught in public schools. So in reality, only privately educated students had much chance of attending college. African Americans faced the added difficulty that many colleges would not accept black students. These inequalities fueled the debate over what should be taught in public schools. Businessmen argued that it was pointless to educate children in ancient languages when they would spend their adult lives working down in the mine or in a factory. For many African Americans, the problem was not just what should be taught; the issue was having any access at all to adequate schooling. In 1932, 230 southern counties had no high schools for African Americans. Ironically, the Depression helped bring about the end of segregation in education. Northern school boards merged schools to save money and in so doing, brought black and white children together. Meanwhile, New Deal agencies helped more than half a million African American adults learn to read and write.

Progressive educators tried to break the cycle of failure that gripped public schools. They campaigned to change college entrance requirements and restructure the school curriculum. Progressives hoped to reform the whole education system. Although the Depression delayed some of their plans, by 1935 improvements in the system had begun. The arguments of those wishing to limit the education of people who might spend their lives toiling in a mine or on a railroad were rejected in favor of equal educational opportunities for all. By the end of the decade, the American public school system was fairer and better run than it had been before.

Charles A. Beard (1874–1948) Born in Indiana, historian and educator Charles A. Beard studied at Oxford University in England and received his Ph.D. from Columbia University in 1904. Leaving Columbia, Beard argued that America was developing into a modern industrial democracy, and that children had to be prepared for change. Although he was not a communist, Beard was denounced as one by the Hearst newspapers. Beard was one of the most influential historians of the 1930s, but during the next decade, he angered many by criticizing Roosevelt's foreign policy and underestimating the warlike intentions of Germany and Japan. *Photo courtesy of the Library of Congress.*

Mary McLeod Bethune (1875–1955) Educator Mary McLeod Bethune was probably the most powerful African American woman in the United States in the 1930s. She founded Bethune-Cookman College in Jacksonville, Mississippi, in 1929, and a decade later it was one of the foremost teacher training colleges in the South. Bethune was a close advisor to Eleanor Roosevelt (1884–1962) and informed her on civil rights. Bethune became the director of Negro Affairs for the National Youth Administration (NYA), an agency that helped young people stay in school or find work. Bethune's efforts there helped more than 150,000 African American teenagers go on to high school. *Photo reproduced by permission of the estate of Carl Van Vechten.*

Horace Mann Bond (1904–1972) Educator Horace Mann Bond's career demonstrates a problem faced by African Americans in the segregated South. Although he despised it, Bond had to work within the segregated system. He used his position as a prominent African American scholar to challenge the idea that blacks were of inferior intelligence than whites. But instead of challenging segregation, Bond worked to make sure that black schools received the same level of funding as white schools. Bond eventually became president of Fort Valley State College in Georgia, and later the first black president of Lincoln University, Pennsylvania.

George S. Counts (1889–1974) George S. Counts made his name arguing that educators held the key to economic prosperity and social reform. He was at the forefront of the debate between conservatives, who wanted students to learn traditional subjects such as Latin and Greek, by traditional methods, and the progressives, who wanted a more critical, open-minded, and experiential approach. Counts was attacked as a communist, but in fact he worked to rid the American Federation of Teachers (AFT) of its communist factions. He wrote several books on academic freedom and worked as a university teacher until 1971. *Photo courtesy of the Library of Congress.*

Catherine Brieger Stern (1894–1973) Catherine Brieger Stern received her Ph.D. in physics and mathematics in 1918, but she also had a strong interest in literature. With her husband, Stern arrived in the United States from Germany in 1938. Her approach to teaching elementary mathematics and reading made her a leader in kindergarten education. As a progressive educator, Stern's method of teaching math involved games, puzzles, and practical activities. She taught reading skills through word games. Stern outlined her approach in several textbooks. Her work had a strong influence on the teaching of those subjects throughout the remainder of the twentieth century.

Loyd S. Tireman (1896–1959) Loyd S. Tireman's work with Spanish-speaking children in New Mexico met with much prejudice and opposition. He had noted in the 1920s that English-speaking children did much better in school than Spanish speakers. In 1930 he began teaching reading skills in English to Hispanic students. His experiments at the school in San Jose, New Mexico, helped other schools in the area to adjust their program to the needs of Hispanics. Most of Tireman's problems came from other educators, who saw Hispanics as racially inferior. Through his work, Tireman challenged the idea that nonwhites should be kept out of mainstream education.

◆◆ *Topics in the News* ·

❖ **PAYING FOR SCHOOL**

The Depression had a huge impact on education, as it did in other areas of American life. The country's public school system had expanded dramatically during the 1920s. In Detroit, Michigan, the number of children in school more than doubled, from 122,690 in 1920 to 250,994 in 1930. The numbers were still rising in 1931, when more American children had access to education than ever before. But school districts had borrowed money to fund expansion, and business leaders wanted their money back as the economy slipped into depression.

School districts were soon struggling with debt. Nationwide, schools owed a total of $93 million in 1930. By 1934, that figure had risen to $137 million. At the same time, revenues had fallen. As the economic situation grew worse, schools closed down, teachers' salaries were cut, fewer subjects were taught, and plans for expansion and reform were shelved. Georgia closed down 1,318 schools in the early 1930s. In Dayton, Ohio, schools opened only three days each week. The art, music, home economics, and physical education classes that had been introduced during the 1920s could no longer be funded. By 1934, the resources spent on each student and the narrow list of subjects offered in the public school system was no better than it had been before World War I.

As funding from businesses and local sources dried up, schools and colleges relied heavily on money from state and federal governments. Although this meant that many school budgets had to be cut, it also made funding fairer. State "foundation grants" ensured that a minimum level of schooling was available to more children. State support for schools doubled between 1930 and 1940 to an average of around 30 percent of the total cost. But state funding could never provide minimum standards across the country because poor states, such as South Carolina, could not afford to spend as much as richer states, such as Delaware.

Federal funding could have helped reduce or remove inequalities, but efforts to finance education from Washington met with opposition. Many lawmakers thought it would destroy the tradition of local control of schools, while southerners thought federal funding would lead to desegregation. Others thought the cost of education would bankrupt the government. It would be another decade before federal funding would have a noticeable effect on the national education system.

Although the Depression put an end to many of the educational advances of the 1920s, it also inspired change and reform. As budgets were cut, schools were given more control over how their money could be spent. The curriculum was reformed, and textbooks and testing were standardized. School districts merged, worked together, and organized themselves to save money. They offered a more consistent and efficient service. Although a well-organized and properly surveyed education system had long been the aim of reformers, it took the hardships of the Depression to make it happen. At the beginning of the 1930s, American schools were in turmoil. By the end of the decade, the entire education system was more modern, more professional, and much fairer.

❖ THE NEW DEAL AND EDUCATION

Because it was such a dangerous political issue, President Franklin D. Roosevelt (1882–1945) left control of schools and colleges to local school boards and governing bodies. New Dealers tried hard not to give the impression that they were trying to move power to Washington. Roosevelt even went so far as to stay away from the National Education Association (NEA) convention in 1934. As a result the relationship between educators and the Roosevelt administration was tense. Federal assistance for schools was disappointing, while the U.S. Office of Education was scaled back. The reasons were mostly political. By funding schools for African Americans, the New Deal would have antagonized southerners. Similarly, public school assistance would upset the Catholic school lobby in big business. The New Deal stayed out of education to protect political allegiances that were important for the rest of the program.

Another reason why educators and New Dealers were at odds was a simple difference in their approach. Before the Depression, most teachers were middle class, conservative, and Protestant, with links to business. They saw their role as being to "elevate" children to their own set of tastes and values. The New Dealers were different. They were interested in mass education, not just for the gifted. They focused on skills, education through experience, and the arts. Where professional educators tended to favor classroom learning, New Dealers exposed students to theater, film, art exhibitions, and writing workshops.

Roosevelt distrusted his education commissioner, John Studebaker (1887–1989). When he and Studebaker disagreed on what to do, New Deal educational programs were pushed through other agencies such as the Tennessee Valley Authority (TVA), the Works Progress Administration (WPA), the Civilian Conservation Corps (CCC), and the National Youth Administration (NYA). Rather than going through Studebaker's department, the Federal Emergency Relief Administration (FERA), run by Harry Hopkins (1890–1946), was used to pay $14 million in teachers' salaries to keep rural schools open. Between 1933 and 1939, 70 percent of new school construction was paid for by the federal government. Thousands of schools were decorated and repaired by the WPA. But Roosevelt avoided financing schools in a direct way. The money always went through New Deal agencies, funding youth and adult education programs in subjects from the liberal arts to agriculture. The aim was to give people "a decent break" by teaching them to read and write, and giving them a chance to go further. Although they annoyed professional educators, New Deal programs proved that learning did not have to be—and indeed, should not be—accessible to the white middle class only.

❖ MORE WORK FOR LESS PAY

When school boards apportioned their new, smaller budgets, teachers' salaries were hit hardest. Between 1929 and 1934, average teachers' pay fell from $1,420 to $1,227 annually, a drop of more than 13 percent. School boards expected teachers to accept the cuts while taking on more work. Knowing that any job was better than no job, most teachers did exactly as they were told. Married women teachers had the most to fear. They often lost their jobs in order to keep men in work. Job losses and low pay made the teachers militant. They formed unions and demonstrated in the streets for better pay and work conditions.

The American Federation of Teachers (AFT) and the National Education Association (NEA) tended to distance themselves from the labor unions. But as salaries fell and school closures accelerated, tension grew

*The Civilian Conservation Corps was a product of Roosevelt's New Deal that put more than three million men back into the workforce. **Courtesy of the Library of Congress.***

between the teachers and administrators. The teachers' associations became more militant as the decade went on. In 1933, twenty thousand teachers, students, and parents went on a march to protest against Chicago's school board and its link with big business. They demonstrated against banks that refused teachers credit, and male teachers fought with the police. The result was that the Chicago school board voted to fire 1,400 teachers. The tangled connection between business and education was especially bad in Chicago, but similar problems existed elsewhere. The AFT and NEA campaigned for a more open, better-managed system of education financing. They were successful at keeping some schools open and protecting teachers' jobs. But as things improved, teachers lost their radical edge. Left-wing AFT president Jerome Davis (1891–1979) was replaced by the anticommunist George Counts (1889–1974) in 1939. Demonstrations and strikes gave way to negotiations for better pensions, pay, and smaller classes.

The economic hardships of the Depression had forced both teachers and schools to be more organized and efficient. Teachers gained more control over their work through unions and new laws aimed at standardizing education. Teachers had to be better qualified, and their performance was monitored, but laws were brought in to give them "tenure," protecting them from dismissal. Professional associations, such as the American Federation of Teachers (AFT) and the National Education Association (NEA), saw a rise in membership despite a drop in the number of teachers.

❖ CHANGING THE WAY AMERICANS ARE TAUGHT

Progressive education was based on the idea that children learn more by experience and observation than they do memorizing facts by heart. Progressivism had become popular in previous decades, but it had very little impact on the schools' curriculum until the early 1930s. University of Chicago philosopher John Dewey (1859–1952) pioneered progressivism at his "laboratory school." In one famous experiment, Dewey had the children build a log cabin. Not only did they learn principles of geometry, but they also found out about homesteading and the history of western expansion and picked up practical skills, as well. Since one traditional method of teaching reading at the time was Bible recitation, Dewey's ideas were shocking to many educators. Dewey believed that schools were at the center of democratic society. When the Depression appeared to threaten democracy, Dewey and his followers looked to the schools to save the American democratic project.

Progressive education gradually began to take hold on the school curriculum. Classes became more "child centered" and vocational. Traditional schooling involved a teacher giving instruction from the front of a class-

"How happy, I am!" said Dick.
"How happy I am!" said Jane.
Grandmother is here.
Grandmother laughed.
"I am happy," she said.
"I am happy to see you."
"Look!" said Grandmother.
is somethi
what is.

A teacher instructs her students in North Dakota in 1937. Courtesy of the Library of Congress.

room. A new type of school created during the Depression broke with this teacher-centered style. These "folk" schools based lessons on discussion and shared learning, rather than instruction and memorizing. Based on a Danish model, folk schools were communities in themselves. They were often integrated, with teachers and students living together and sharing duties such as cleaning, fundraising, and the running of the school. Folk schools offered courses in political reform, labor organizing, and civil rights. They also helped collect folk music and ran oral history projects. As their name suggests, folk schools put local communities and the experiences of "ordinary" people at the heart of their curriculum. Highlander Folk School in Monteagle, Tennessee, is the most famous of the folk schools. It ran official courses for the Congress of Industrial Organizations (CIO). Like other folk schools, Highlander was attacked by conservatives, who saw such activities as communistic and dangerous.

But in the aftermath of the Depression, many progressive educators took an even more radical approach. Known as "social reconstructionism," this approach involved using education to inform students about the failures of capitalism. In part, social reconstructionism grew out of frustration with conservatives on school boards and in business. Social reconstructionists saw schools as the only area of life that could change society without violence and demonstration. They aimed to change school and college curricula to reflect their views. George S. Counts (1889–1974), one of the movement's leading activists, accused progressivism's conservative opponents of being responsible for the Depression.

Social reconstructionism was opposed by many progressive educators, as well as by conservatives. Both groups believed schools should be run like businesses, and that the Depression was an opportunity to make schools more efficient. Social reconstructionists were described as "romantic" and "sentimental" for believing that child-centered learning could change society. Even Dewey himself sometimes criticized social reconstructionists. He did not believe, as they did, that children would teach themselves, and he did not think that children should be told about only one political point of view. The whole point of progressive education, Dewey thought, was to expose children to many different views and ideas. By the end of the 1930s, social reconstructionism had gone out of favor, but progressive education, although its name disappeared, had brought profound changes to the character of American education.

❖ TRAINING ADULTS

Labor colleges were set up and supported by labor unions to train union activists, lawyers, and journalists. Labor colleges also offered a traditional education for people who had missed out on schooling when they were children. Industrial workers, farmers, and the unemployed all benefited from a labor college education. Although most labor colleges had been set up in the 1920s or earlier, during the Depression they became an important feature of the American education system. They taught unusual economic theories, encouraged community life, and published pamphlets on union organizing and politics. Faculty and students often worked on behalf of the unions. They promoted union causes and handed out leaflets at meetings. So-called "agitprop" theater came out of the labor colleges. "Agitprop" is a combination of the words "agitating" and "propaganda." It was a form of theater that tried to inform its audience of important political issues and "agitate" them into action. Because of their left-wing politics, labor colleges came in for attack from conservatives, who accused them of supporting communist values.

Many labor college graduates went on to become prominent union leaders. One of the most notable labor college graduates was Walter Reuther (1907–1970). Reuther attended Brookwood Labor College in Duluth, Minnesota (founded 1903). He was one of the organizers of the 1936 sit-down strike at General Motors. Despite their success, labor colleges gradually ran out of money or fell into dispute with the unions. Brookwood closed in 1937, Commonwealth College in 1940, and Work People's College in 1941.

Women also benefited from new educational opportunities. Bennington College was set up in 1932 to provide college education especially for women. It drew on several financial sources, including the town of Bennington, Vermont, where it was situated. Bennington encouraged individualism in its students. What made Bennington different from traditional college was its "learning by doing" approach. In the twenty-first century, most colleges have artists, writers, and musicians on the faculty. But when Bennington opened, this was a new idea, and it was soon emulated in other schools. Choreographer Martha Graham (1894–1991) was among the first of many artists to teach at Bennington. Black Mountain College, in North Carolina, also attracted some of the most creative people of the period as teachers. Architect Buckminster Fuller (1895–1983) taught there, as did artist Willem de Kooning (1904–1997) and social critic Paul Goodman (1911–1972). Other small colleges offering experimental education included Rollins College in Winter Park, Florida, Antioch College in Yellow Springs, Ohio, and Swarthmore College, near Philadelphia. While not all of them survived long in their original form, these small colleges succeeded in changing the way schools, colleges, and universities delivered their programs.

❖ ACADEMIC FREEDOM UNDER ATTACK

The principle of academic freedom allows teachers to do their job without interference from politicians or other powerful interest groups. It enables them to teach important subjects or points of view even when they might be unpopular with those in power. When educators began to campaign for better pay and conditions in schools, conservative politicians and citizen groups went on the attack. Pressure groups such as the American Legion and the Daughters of the American Revolution (DAR) accused teachers of being communists. When the Democrats won their second term in Congress in 1936, strengthening political support for progressive education, conservatives focused their efforts on trying to reverse the trend in individual schools. Conservatives feared that public schools were filling children's minds with communist ideals, and they tried to prevent teachers from discussing progressive ideas.

Conservatives were anxious about progressive education, which valued discussion and argument in the classroom over learning lists of facts. They believed communists were trying to take over schools. Anyone who didn't agree with them was labeled a "red." As early as 1928, the Daughters of the American Revolution (DAR) accused the National Education Association (NEA) of being "sympathetic to communist ideals." With the Depression came even more attacks, especially when teachers campaigned against cutbacks. Elizabeth Dilling's book *The Red Network* (1936) is a "who's who" of people she suspected of being communists. The people listed range from schoolteachers to President Roosevelt himself.

"Red baiting," as it was called, was also used to sell newspapers. The Hearst Press ran a campaign against "reds" on the front pages of its newspapers. The owner of the press, William Randolph Hearst (1863–1951), allowed papers to publish editorials and articles that denounced teachers. The school boards even attacked their own employees, dismissing their complaints about salary cuts as a communist plot. Red baiting was common throughout the education system. The New York State Economic Council declared that the history textbooks of Harold Rugg (1886–1960) promoted "unrest." Rugg's respected and popular books were used in more than 4,200 school systems at the time. In Illinois, in 1935, Charles Walgreen (1873–1939), the drugstore chain owner, persuaded the state legislature to investigate communism at the University of Chicago. No evidence of subversive activity was found.

Not all attacks on academic freedom came from conservatives. Many high-ranking officials in the teacher unions *were* communists. They campaigned for equality for black students and were dedicated to modernizing the American school system. But the Communist Party also wanted to take over the teacher unions and promote the cause of the Soviet Union. Communist takeover bids upset noncommunists within the organizations. During the 1930s, teachers came under pressure from the school boards, the press, the bankers, and communist members of their own unions.

Academic freedom was also challenged by the need for teachers to swear loyalty oaths. Beginning in the 1920s, some states required teachers to swear not to mention "subversive" ideas in the classroom. The term "subversive" covered a wide range of things, from Marxism to sexual liberation and civil rights. The penalty for refusing to sign a loyalty oath was dismissal. By 1936, twenty-one states had loyalty oaths. Many states also made children say the pledge of allegiance at the start of the school day. This was declared unconstitutional in the 1940s. The oath that caused most controversy was the "red rider." This rider to a congressional appropriation bill forced teachers in Washington, D.C., to sign a statement saying they would not teach communism. Teachers pointed out that they were being required to sign away their constitutional right to freedom of expression. Under pressure from teachers, the rider was dropped in 1937.

❖ AFRICAN AMERICAN EDUCATION

Nationally, more than one-quarter of the students in the 1930s were black. Yet they received only about one-tenth of the total education revenues. Many Americans believed that African Americans were simply not capable of excelling in school. Georgia education officials argued that blacks were "a thousand years" behind whites in the development of their brains. In the South, where segregation was the law, African Americans attended poorly funded schools with fewer teachers and books than white schools. Education officials often used these students' poor scores to "prove" the inferiority of the black intellect. Yet very few students of any race could learn and excel academically under such conditions.

In the North, although it was not legally enforced, segregation was the norm. African Americans lived in different areas from whites; rarely did they attend the same public schools. In the North, the schools attended by black students were not as well funded as those attended by whites because black communities were not as wealthy as white ones. Funding for schools in the South was also unequal, but southern school boards further perpetuated the inequities by refusing to repair, improve, or build new schools for black children, even though they were simultaneously pouring funds into white schools.

African Americans could rely only on their own communities to change their children's educational opportunities. In the 1920s and early 1930s, they began to organize self-help groups to build and repair schools. The whole community was involved. Elderly sharecroppers, many born into slavery, donated their life savings to see their grandchildren educated. Communal farms donated profits to school projects. Even people with no children donated money, sometimes mortgaging their homes to raise cash. Those without money gave their time and skills. Carpenters and builders spent their free time building schools, while women prepared food for the builders and ran fundraising events. Sometimes wealthy white families gave money. Julius Rosenwald (1862–1932), chairman of Sears, Roebuck, and Company, was one prominent contributor. On average, self-help projects raised around 90 percent of the capital they needed from within black communities. By 1932, self-help groups had built 3,464 schools in counties across the South.

Although the self-help school building program had many successes, it was not enough. Only one-quarter of black children had access to a school in the early 1930s, and most of those were elementary schools.

*OPPOSITE PAGE
African American children attended schools with poor management and low funding. Segregated schools were legal until 1954. Reproduced by permission of the Corbis Corporation.*

Only 19 percent of African Americans aged fourteen to nineteen were in high school. There were almost no high schools for them in rural areas, and no transportation to take them there if they lived too far away to walk. In contrast, almost all whites in rural areas had access to high schools, whether they chose to attend or not.

Instead of a broad liberal education, covering mathematics, literature, and history, African Americans were offered "industrial education." This was really just training for low-paying industrial jobs. Industrial high schools taught carpentry, auto mechanics, bricklaying, sewing, cooking,

and metalworking. These are all useful skills, but they didn't give black students the opportunity to break out of low-paid jobs or to reach their full potential. African Americans wanted traditional education and the chance to go to college. But by 1939 there was such a severe shortage of traditional high schools for African Americans that few could attend college.

The Depression put an end to most self-help projects, and white-run school boards had even less money to spend on black schools. Although volunteers in Louisiana donated labor worth $2,947 to school projects in 1933, teacher salaries, books, and transportation had to be paid for with cash. Teachers wrote letters begging for donations, but they rarely resulted in much financial assistance. Yet not everything in education was so bad for African Americans. Black colleges—for the students who could attend them—did well in the 1930s, supported mostly by well-off white benefactors. New Deal agencies, such as the National Youth Administration, gave instruction in academic subjects as well as industrial arts and domestic service.

The 1930s marked the beginning of desegregation in American education. In northern cities, desegregation was achieved by several methods. The Educational Equality League of Philadelphia campaigned publicly for desegregation, for more black teachers, and for an African American member of the city's school board. The National Association for the Advancement of Colored People (NAACP) went to court to challenge segregation. The NAACP knew a direct challenge was unlikely to succeed, so it fought individual cases. In 1936 the NAACP fought for Donald Murray's right to be admitted to the law school at the University of Maryland. The court ruled that the university should admit Murray, or build a separate law school for him. Murray was admitted. Despite such cases, it would take more than twenty more years of struggle before African Americans in the South could claim a legal right to the same education as whites, and it would be years beyond that before school districts stopped actively circumventing the law to prevent them from exercising their education rights.

For More Information

BOOKS

Berube, Maurice R. *Teacher Politics: The Influence of Unions.* New York: Greenwood Press, 1988.

Bowen, David J. *The Struggle Within: Race Relations in the United States.* New York: Grosset and Dunlap, 1972.

Cobb, William H. *Radical Education in the Rural South: Commonwealth College 1923–1940.* Detroit: Wayne State University Press, 2000.

OPPOSITE PAGE
A school desegregation protest in St. Louis, Missouri, in 1933.

Collier, Christopher, and James Lincoln Collier. *Progressivism, the Great Depression, and the New Deal, 1901 to 1941.* New York: Benchmark Books/Marshall Cavendish, 2001.

Dilling, Elizabeth. *The Red Network.* Chicago, 1936.

Eaton, William Edward. *The American Federation of Teachers, 1916–1961: A History of the Movement.* Carbondale: Southern Illinois University Press, 1975.

Farrell, Jacqueline. *The Great Depression.* San Diego, CA: Lucent Books, 1996.

Feinstein, Stephen. *The 1930s: From the Great Depression to the Wizard of Oz (Decades of the Twentieth Century).* New York: Enslow Publishers, 2001.

Haskins, James. *Separate, but Not Equal: The Dream and the Struggle.* New York: Scholastic, 1998.

Isaacs, Sally Senzell. *America in the Time of Franklin Delano Roosevelt: The Story of Our Nation from Coast to Coast, from 1929 to 1948.* Des Plaines, IL: Heinemann Library, 2000.

Lindsay, Paul. *Breaking the Bonds of Racism.* Homewood, IL: ETC Publications, 1974.

Lusane, Clarence. *The Struggle for Equal Education.* New York: F. Watts, 1992.

Nishi, Dennis. *Life During the Great Depression.* San Diego, CA: Lucent Books, 1998.

Rensberger, Susan. *A Multicultural Portrait of the Great Depression.* Tarrytown, NY: Benchmark Books, 1996.

Sherrow, Victoria. *Hardship and Hope: America and the Great Depression.* New York: Twenty-First Century Books, 1997.

Trotter, Joe William. *From a Raw Deal to a New Deal?: African Americans, 1929–1945.* New York: Oxford University Press, 1996.

Wroble, Lisa. *Kids During the Great Depression.* New York: Powerkids Press, 1999.

WEB SITES

Consortium of Vermont Colleges: Bennington. http://www.vtcolleges.org/vtcolleges/benc/ (accessed July 23, 2002).

The History of Education and Childhood: International archive of links and source materials on the history of education & the history of childhood. http://www.socsci.kun.nl/ped/whp/histeduc/index.html (accessed July 23, 2002).

Student Activism in the 1930s. http://newdeal.feri.org/students/captions.htm (accessed July 23, 2002).

Schools as Social Regulators, 1920s and 1930s Homepage. http://www.bc.edu/bc_org/avp/soe/te/pages/docstudwork/ed711/pages/regulator1.html (accessed July 23, 2002).

Wofford, Andy. *The Rural South in the 1930s.* http://dsl.snet.net/features/issues/articles/2000/10270101.shtml (accessed July 23, 2002).

Government, Politics, and Law

1930: **January** Nationwide unemployment reaches four million.

1930: **February 10** More than one hundred people are arrested in Chicago for bootlegging (the illegal selling of alcoholic beverages).

1930: **June 17** The Smoot-Hawley Tariff Act sets the highest import tariffs (taxes on imported goods) in American history.

1930: **December 11** The Bank of the United States closes, taking with it the savings of more than 400,000 depositors.

1931: **January 7** A government report informs President Herbert Hoover that almost five million Americans are out of work.

1931: **January 19** "Prohibition is not working," claims a government report from the Wickersham Committee on Law Enforcement and Observance.

1931: **March 3** Hoover signs a bill making "The Star Spangled Banner" the national anthem.

1932: **February** The Reconstruction Finance Corporation and the Glass-Steagall Credit Expansion Act allow businesses to borrow money to keep people in work. In all almost two billion dollars of loans and gold reserves are made available.

1932: **November 8** Franklin D. Roosevelt is elected to his first term as president of the United States.

1933: **March 5** In an attempt to stop the banking crisis, Roosevelt declares a four-day national bank holiday.

1933: **March 9** The first "hundred days" of the "First New Deal" begins with a special session of Congress that concentrates on passing legislation to revive the economy.

1933: **March 12** Roosevelt makes his first "fireside chat" on national radio.

1933: **June 16** The first "hundred days" of the New Deal ends with fifteen major pieces of legislation in place, including the National Industrial Recovery Act (NIRA).

1933: **June 16** Banks are forbidden to sell stocks and bonds by the Glass-Steagall Banking Act. The Federal Deposit Insurance Corporation insures banks against failure.

1933: **December 5** Prohibition ends with the Twenty-first Amendment to the Constitution, which repeals the Eighteenth Amendment.

1934: **January 30** The Gold Reserve Act allows the government greater control over the value of the currency.

1934: **February 15** The Civil Works Emergency Relief Act authorizes $950 million in funding for civil works projects.

1934: **April 28** The Homeowners' Loan Act helps people buy their own homes or reorganize their mortgages in order to boost the building industry.

1934: **June 28** The Frazier-Lemke Farm Bankruptcy Act stops banks from foreclosing on loans to farmers for five years. The Taylor Grazing Act aims to help prevent soil erosion.

1934: **November 6** Democrats gain nine seats in both the Senate and House of Representatives.

1935: **January 4** The "Second New Deal" begins with Roosevelt's plans for social reform.

1935: **April 8** The Works Progress Administration (WPA) is created. It will eventually employ eight million people in building works and public arts projects.

1935: **May 27** The NIRA is declared unconstitutional by the Supreme Court.

1935: **July 5** After the failure of NIRA in the courts, the National Labor Relations Act (Wagner Act) restores the right of workers to form unions.

1936: **November 3** Franklin D. Roosevelt is elected to his second term as president.

1937: **February 5** Roosevelt announces his intention to increase the number of Supreme Court justices to fifteen. He is attacked for trying to influence the court's decisions through "court packing."

1937: **March 1** The Supreme Court Retirement Act allows justices to retire at age seventy on full pay. In the months that follow, the Supreme Court upholds several key New Deal measures, including the minimum wage for women and the Social Security Act.

1938: **January 3** President Roosevelt's State of the Union address declares the need to build up the nation's military defenses.

1938: **May 26** The House Un-American Activities Committee (HUAC) is established.

1938: **June 25** Forty-four hours is set as the federal standard work week by the Fair Labor Standards Act.

1938: **November 14** The United States recalls its ambassador from Germany in protest of the treatment of Jews.

1939: **January 5** More than $1 billion in defense spending is demanded in the budget.

1939: **April 14** Roosevelt calls for a world disarmament conference and appeals to Adolf Hitler of Germany and Benito Mussolini of Italy to act peacefully.

1939: **September 1** Germany invades Poland, beginning World War II.

1939: **September 5** Roosevelt declares the United States neutral in the war in Europe.

Overview

The 1930s were dominated by the Great Depression, the biggest economic crisis the nation had ever known. Unlike economic crises of the past, the Great Depression was long lasting and touched almost every area of American life. Understandably, the government of the United States was driven between 1930 and 1939 by the need to end the crisis and to make sure it never happened again. Republicans and Democrats each had their own ideas about how to go about achieving those goals. The country also had small, vocal groups of socialists, communists, American fascists, and Nazi sympathizers, all of whom added to the debates. The sheer number of voices trying to be heard made the 1930s a dramatic decade in American politics.

Herbert Hoover became president in 1929. The 1920s had been a period of prosperity, and he inherited an economy that was outwardly strong. But within a few months, cracks started appearing. The stock market crash of October 29, 1929, triggered a chain reaction. Unemployment rose dramatically, prices fell, and banks began to go out of business. At first, Hoover and his Republican advisers believed that the markets would correct themselves. Hoover met with business leaders to persuade them not to lay off workers and not to cut wages. He initiated higher tariffs (taxes on imported goods) to protect American business from foreign competition. But in 1932, with unemployment over 23 percent, and no sign of improvement on the way, Hoover changed his policy. He put in place what was then the largest peacetime spending program in American history. The Reconstruction Finance Corporation (RFC) made more than $1 billion available to business in the form of loans. Yet even that was not enough to save either the economy or Hoover's presidency. Franklin D. Roosevelt won the election for the Democrats in autumn of the same year.

Where the Republican administration had avoided interfering with the economy, Roosevelt favored taking direct action. For several years the United States had suffered poverty, homelessness, and great hardship. In his inaugural speech, Roosevelt promised a "New Deal" for Americans. The First New Deal (a set of government programs launched between 1933 and 1935) was aimed at the immediate problems of unemployment, homelessness, and the economy. In its first one hundred days, the administration poured billions of dollars into relief programs and job creation schemes, as well as plans to deal with the banking and farm crises. The Second New Deal (1935–37) marked a turn to the political left. At the center of the second phase was the Social Security Act of 1935. For the first time, unemployment insurance, public housing, and social security payments were available for those unable to fend for themselves. In his second term, Roosevelt would encounter problems as the economy continued to falter. But New Deal policies were responsible for lifting the American economy out of the slump and preparing it for the future. Roosevelt built a coalition of labor unions, women, African Americans, ethnic groups, and the middle class that redefined American politics and lasted until the 1960s.

Besides economic and political change, the 1930s also saw a change in attitude toward civil rights. Racism was deeply rooted in many areas of American life, and Roosevelt wanted to solve the growing problem. Unfortunately, the New Dealers had to back down from some proposed civil rights legislation in order to avoid breaking up their fragile political coalition. One area of social reform that did succeed was the repeal of Prohibition. By 1932, the American public had lost the will to maintain a legal ban on alcoholic drinks, mostly because the law had been so difficult to enforce. Although organized crime received less publicity after the 1933 repeal, it continued to spread to areas of business other than the production and sale of alcohol as the Depression took hold of the country.

The major international political issue late in the decade was the start of war in Europe. In 1937 there was widespread support for "isolationism" in the United States. An opinion poll found that 64 percent of Americans favored staying out of the growing conflict in Europe. In the next few years, however, Hitler's Germany became more troublesome, and relations with Japan grew tense. Support for isolationism began to fade. As the 1930s drew to a close, the United States built up its navy and armed forces and prepared for war.

"Ma" Barker (1871–1935) Born as Arizona Clark, "Ma" Barker struggled to raise her four sons in Springfield, Missouri. From 1932 onward, after the eldest son, Herman, killed himself while escaping the police, the Barker gang organized several kidnappings. The boys were more than willing to execute their enemies, and Barker sheltered several wanted men in the early 1930s. Barker's career, and her life, ended during a four-hour shootout at Lake Weir, Florida. Doubt remains over whether Ma Barker was a gang leader or just an overprotective mother looking after her wayward "boys." *Photo reproduced by permission of the Corbis Corporation.*

Herbert Hoover (1874–1964) The stock market crash of 1929 came less than a year into Herbert Hoover's presidency. Hoover's "hands-off" policies failed to help the suffering of the American people. He became known as a president who didn't care and lost his bid for re-election. But despite his reputation in office, Hoover was a caring and sensitive man. During World War I he was responsible for distributing food and clothing to troubled European nations. Later in his career Hoover headed several government commissions. *Photo courtesy of the Library of Congress.*

J. Edgar Hoover (1895–1972) Beginning in the 1920s, J. Edgar Hoover turned the Bureau of Investigation (known as the Federal Bureau of Investigation, or FBI, starting in 1935) into the nation's most powerful police force. In the 1930s, it was at the center of the New Deal's war on crime. Hoover's Bureau began to centralize crime records and build itself into a formidable and popular weapon against organized crime. But the FBI was also used for political ends, investigating government employees using wiretaps and break-ins. Hoover's power grew with the secrets he collected, and the FBI developed a shadowy reputation that survived for decades. *Photo reproduced by permission of Archive Photos, Inc.*

Alf Landon (1887–1987) Alf Landon spent most of his life working in politics. In the 1920s, he worked closely with William Allen White (1868–1944) in his anti-Ku Klux Klan campaign, and he governed Kansas during most of the 1930s. Landon is best known for his run for president against FDR in 1936. He took on the popular president with little hope of winning. As Governor of Kansas from 1932, Landon had been an important Republican supporter of the New Deal. But in the 1936 presidential election, Americans showed they preferred Roosevelt's handling of the economy as a Democrat. Landon carried only two states, with eight electoral college votes, as compared to Roosevelt's 523. *Photo reproduced by permission of the Corbis Corporation.*

Huey P. Long (1893–1935) In his time as governor, charismatic Huey P. Long became known as the "dictator of Louisiana." He served as both the governor and a senator for the state. Once, when an opponent argued that he was in breach of the constitution, Long retorted: "I'm the constitution round here." He built many bridges, schools, and other buildings, but in 1929 he was impeached on corruption charges. He was never convicted. A critic of the New Deal because he didn't think it went far enough, Long's Share-Our-Wealth Society promised to divide up the nation's wealth equally. He was assassinated in the Louisiana State Capitol building.

Frances Perkins (1882–1965) Frances Perkins was the first woman to hold a cabinet post in the U.S. government. Born in Boston, she trained as a teacher and worked as a volunteer with the poor of Chicago. She held important posts in New York State government, fighting for shorter working days and safer conditions. As U.S. Secretary of Labor, Perkins developed the Civilian Conservation Corps and the National Industrial Recovery Act, as well as helping to craft the Social Security Act (1935). After Roosevelt's death in 1945, she served for twenty years on the Civil Service Commission. *Photo reproduced by permission of Archive Photos, Inc.*

Eleanor Roosevelt (1884–1962) Known as "the conscience of the White House" during the presidency of her husband, Eleanor Roosevelt was a powerful influence on the politics of the 1930s. Although she believed women needed special protection at work and opposed the Equal Rights Amendment, she was an outspoken defender of women's rights. She also promoted civil rights, resigning her membership in the Daughters of the American Revolution because of their racism. From January 1936, she wrote "My Day," a popular syndicated newspaper column discussing political issues. At her death, she was hailed as the "First Lady of the World." *Photo reproduced by permission of AP/Wide World Photos.*

◆◆◆◆ *Topics in the News* •

❖ THE AGONY OF THE GREAT DEPRESSION

By 1930, as the Great Depression became a serious problem across the United States, millions of Americans had lost their jobs, their homes, and their life savings. The national government didn't seem to care. As Americans became more desperate, people began to take action for themselves. In Arkansas, an armed crowd of five hundred farmers marched on the town of England and looted its stores for food. In 1933, Nebraska farmers forced their way past police barricades to march on the state capitol and demand debt relief. In Iowa, farmers fought with police until the governor sent in troopers to impose martial law. But it was the veterans' "bonus march" that had the biggest impact at a national level.

In 1924, veterans of World War I had been offered a bonus payment, to be claimed in full in 1945. In the depths of the Depression, that seemed a long time to wait for many veterans. In 1932, Congressman Wright Patman (1893–1976) tried to push through a bill allowing early payment. A group of veterans calling themselves the "Bonus Expeditionary Force" marched on Washington, D.C., in support. During the summer, around sixteen thousand men camped on vacant land along the Potomac River, near the Capitol. When the Patman bill failed in the Senate on June 17,

The Bonus Army protested army veterans' loss of benefits, one of the many financial losses of the Great Depression. Here, shacks built by the Bonus Army burn after a battle with the military in 1932. Reproduced by permission of the National Archives and Records Administration.

	Presidential Candidate	Political Party	Electoral College Votes	Popular Votes Cast
1932	Franklin D. Roosevelt	Democrat	472	22,829,501
	Herbert C. Hoover	Republican	59	15,760,684
	Norman Thomas	Socialist	0	884,649
	William Z. Foster	Communist	0	103,253
1936	Franklin D. Roosevelt	Democrat	523	27,757,333
	Alfred M. Landon	Republican	8	16,684,231
	William Lemke	Union	0	892,267
	Norman Thomas	Socialist	0	187,833

Source: Cook, Chris, and David Waller, eds. *The Longman Handbook of Modern American History 1763–1996*. Harlow, UK: Longman, 1998.

1932, tension began to rise. Veterans refused to leave their camps, and police moved in. Squatters in a Treasury Department building on Pennsylvania Avenue were attacked, and two were killed. Chief of Staff General Douglas MacArthur (1880–1964) was sent to assess the camps, but instead sent in cavalry troops, who charged the crowd with drawn sabers. Demonstrators fought back, and it took two days to round them up. President Herbert Hoover (1874–1964) was held responsible for the riot and the display of force. His treatment of the veterans turned many voters against him in the autumn election, as did the widespread opinion that Hoover didn't care about the plight of the common man. When President Franklin D. Roosevelt (1882–1945) faced a similar bonus march in 1935, he offered the protesters accommodation, food, and entertainment.

❖ THE TRIUMPH OF PROGRESSIVISM

Franklin D. Roosevelt (1882–1945) won the 1932 presidential election by a landslide. With almost twenty-three million votes, he bested Hoover's total by more than seven million. Such a lead in the popular vote gave Roosevelt, who was known as FDR, the opportunity to make many changes. As a progressive (one who believed that the power of the government should be used to ensure progress), FDR had crafted "New Deal" policies that were very similar to the policies of his distant cousin, Theodore Roosevelt (1858–1919), who was the U.S. president from 1901 to 1909. In 1912, during Woodrow Wilson's presidency, Theodore Roosevelt's Progressive Party had called for a scheme to protect workers from poverty in case of illness or unemployment. It had demanded fairer taxation, protection for the unions, regulation of trade between states, and an end to child labor. These goals were all achieved by FDR and the New Deal in the 1930s.

Prior to the 1932 election, Roosevelt gathered together a group of advisers. The "Brains Trust," as they were known, was made up of Raymond Moley, Rexford G. Tugwell, and Adolf Berle. These three Columbia University professors, led by Moley (1886–1975), prepared speeches and advised on policy. Moley encouraged Roosevelt to give the federal government a more active role in running the country and to borrow money in order to kick-start the economy. Moley's spending plan became the Federal Emergency Relief Administration (FERA), which paid money to the homeless and unemployed. Tugwell (1891–1979) was responsible for farm policy, though he never achieved his dream of persuading Americans to give up on capitalism. Berle (1895–1971) helped develop the Reconstruction Finance Corporation and schemes to protect farmers and homeowners when they couldn't pay their mortgages. Roosevelt's "take-charge" approach was quite different from the Hoover administration's "hands-off" style. Under Roosevelt, the federal government became a much more powerful, and obvious, influence on American life.

❖ REGULATING THE ECONOMY

With the near collapse of the American banking system in 1932 and 1933, many states had already declared local "banking holidays" to stop people from withdrawing their savings. After his inauguration on March 4, 1933, President Roosevelt took the first decisive action of his presidency on March 9, declaring a national four-day bank holiday. While Congress was in special session, the Emergency Banking Act was passed. Three days later, in his first "fireside chat" on national radio, Roosevelt reassured Americans that the banks would recover. His first act as president was also his first New Deal success. The bank holiday eventually ran for eight days and ended the banking crisis.

Roosevelt's banking reforms did not end there. From January 1933, Ferdinand Pecora (1882–1971) headed an investigation uncovering corruption and fraud among some of the most respectable of American bankers. J. P. Morgan (1867–1943) had a list of "preferred customers" who bought securities from him at below market rate. Morgan then issued the

The New Deal's Alphabet Soup

Roosevelt set up so many New Deal agencies that they were known as an "alphabet soup." Some of the most important of these agencies:

AAA: The Agricultural Adjustment Administration began in May 1933. It paid farmers to plow in crops and destroy animals in order to force prices up.

CCC: The Civilian Conservation Corps started on March 31, 1933. In more than nine years it employed 2.5 million young men to plant trees, fight forest fires, clean reservoirs, and create parks. 35,000 young men were taught to read and write, but women were excluded from joining.

CWA: Devised by FERA director Harry Hopkins (1890–1946) with a budget of almost one billion dollars, the Civil Works Administration gave temporary jobs to more than four million people within thirty days of being approved by Congress in November 1933.

FERA: The Federal Emergency Relief Administration began work on May 22, 1933, giving cash grants to the unemployed.

PWA: The Public Works Administration offered work on government projects to the unemployed. It built hospitals, power plants, and housing projects.

TVA: The Tennessee Valley Authority. One of the great successes of the New Deal, the TVA was established on May 18, 1933. It built a series of dams on the Tennessee River to generate electricity for the region. The Rural Electrification Administration (REA) of 1935 followed the TVA's success, bringing electricity to farms across the country.

WPA: The biggest of all the New Deal agencies, the Works Progress Administration had a budget of five billion dollars, making it the most expensive government program in U.S. history. It employed men building schools and hospitals and renovating bridges and roads. Women worked in childcare or in sewing and traditional crafts. The WPA also paid writers and artists to produce public artworks.

bulk of the securities at a higher rate, giving the first owners instant profit. One of the "preferred customers" was former U.S. president Calvin Coolidge (1872–1933). The Pecora investigation led to legislation to protect the public from the banking industry. The Glass-Steagall act of 1933 made it illegal for banks to deal in stocks and shares and set up the Feder-

Social Security

The Social Security Act (SSA) became law on August 14, 1935. For the first time in American history, the SSA provided a small monthly pension for Americans over the age of sixty-five. It also paid unemployment compensation but was intended as a forced savings plan rather than a true welfare system. After the initial funding was gone, Americans could only collect their pension after a lifetime of social security payments. The SSA was the basis for the American welfare system until 1996.

al Deposit Insurance Corporation (FDIC). The FDIC protected depositors from bank failures and continues to do so in the twenty-first century. Humorist Will Rogers (1879–1935) quipped that Roosevelt made banking so simple even the bankers could understand it.

When Franklin D. Roosevelt (1882–1945) became president in 1933, urgent steps had to be taken to revive the American economy. His "First New Deal" concentrated on passing legislation that would revive the economy. The National Industrial Recovery Act (NIRA), passed by Congress in June 1933, was one of the broadest examples. The NIRA was designed to stop the collapse in prices and rescue American industry. It included many important reforms. It suspended the antitrust laws that prevented businesses from fixing prices among themselves. The NIRA also established the Public Works Administration (PWA) and gave legal protection to labor unions. Through the National Recovery Administration (NRA) and its director Hugh S. Johnson (1882–1942) the NIRA set up a minimum wage, established maximum working hours, and put an end to child labor. Companies that met NRA standards were allowed to display a "Blue Eagle" sign with the slogan "We Do Our Part." A new National Football League franchise in Philadelphia was named the Eagles after the NRA emblem. In May 1935, the U.S. Supreme Court declared the NIRA unconstitutional. Nevertheless, the labor and union reforms of the NIRA were reintroduced later that year as part of the Wagner National Labor Relations Act.

❖ CIVIL RIGHTS

The success of the New Deal depended on several conflicting interest groups working together. The most strained relationship was between

During the 1930s, there were too many people wanting to practice law. Between 1932 and 1937, nine thousand new lawyers graduated from law school each year. This was at a time when business failures and low earnings meant fewer people needed their services. It is estimated that during the Depression years, the amount of legal work available dropped by 70 percent. Law schools, and the American Bar Association (ABA), took steps to limit the number of people qualified to practice law. The ABA used its influence to establish standards for approved law schools. Between 1928 and 1935, the number of students studying at non-approved law schools fell by ten thousand. At the same time, many attorneys and law professors took jobs with New Deal agencies, further reducing the number of lawyers in private or commercial practice.

African Americans and white racists. Discrimination against African Americans was acceptable to most whites in the 1930s. President Roosevelt (1882–1945) depended on the votes of both of these groups to win a second term, and it is for this reason that the New Deal did very little to improve civil rights for blacks. New Dealers even opposed the introduction of anti-lynching laws meant to protect blacks from being killed by white racists. But although the New Deal did very little in terms of action, it did mark the beginning of a change in attitude. African Americans were appointed to senior positions in the administration. Educator Mary McLeod Bethune (1875–1955) became a director of the National Youth Administration, while William Hastie (1904–1976) was an important legal adviser. Robert Weaver (1907–1997), a noted economist, was the first black member of an American cabinet.

❖ THE LIMITS OF ROOSEVELT'S POWER: THE COURT-PACKING PLAN

The expansion of the power of the federal government in the 1930s met with opposition in the courts. Many New Deal programs were threatened by court decisions ruling them unconstitutional. The National Industrial Recovery Act had been rejected and the Agriculture Adjustment Act had been made unworkable by Supreme Court rulings. In order to save the New Deal, Roosevelt fixed on a plan to pack the Supreme Court with judges and officials sympathetic to the New Deal, though he presented it as a plan to reduce the workload for individual judges. On February 5, 1937, his proposals to reform the federal courts went before Congress. Unfortunately, Roosevelt had misjudged the mood of Congress and the electorate. Many state legislatures rejected the scheme, while conservative Democrats also turned against the president. The Supreme Court stood for stability, fairness, and justice. An attack on the Court was an attack on American democracy itself.

Roosevelt struggled to win people over to his ideas for reforming the federal courts. According to Roosevelt, the conservative justices were holding back important reforms that would help millions of Americans. But in fact the federal courts were beginning to change anyway. The Supreme Court Retirement Act of March 1937 allowed justices to retire at age seventy with full pay. Within four years, Roosevelt filled seven vacancies in the Supreme Court. More importantly, the court made several decisions between March and May 1937 that were in the president's favor. These included upholding the Social Security Act and the Wagner Labor Relations Act. The Court became less inclined to rule in favor of the states against the federal government, and this change in judicial direction would lead to the expansion of civil rights after World War II.

❖ U.S. FOREIGN POLICY AND ISOLATIONISM

In the 1930s, American foreign policy was a mixture of efforts to stabilize the world economy and attempts to stay out of international affairs. Before 1933, President Herbert Hoover (1874–1964) tried to calm the international situation, but when the World Disarmament Conference failed to reach agreement in 1932, international tensions began to rise. Germany, Italy, and Japan became more aggressive, while the Soviet Union was a natural enemy of the United States because of its political system. Early in his presidency, Franklin D. Roosevelt (1882–1945) found it easier to keep to the margins of international politics. Although he negotiated trade agreements to protect the interests of American industry abroad, Roosevelt took an "isolationist" position. His priority was to solve the crisis at home.

Isolationists argued that the United States should stay out of foreign conflicts or the affairs of other nations. It was a view held by people from many different political parties; most Americans in the 1930s held isolationist views. The "Good Neighbor Policy" of 1933, which ended many years of U.S. military actions in South America, was essentially an isolationist policy. Secretary of State Cordell Hull (1871–1955) developed the policy, arguing that no nation has the right to interfere in the affairs of another. But critics noted that as the United States withdrew from military action, South American countries were more willing to allow American businesses to exploit their people and natural resources. Many saw isolationist policies as an excuse for the United States to exercise economic power.

President Roosevelt held isolationist views when he began his first term. With the Depression to deal with, and the New Deal to pay for, military action overseas was an unnecessary distraction. The Nye Investigating Committee, led by Senator Gerald Nye (1892–1971), suggested that the country had been led into World War I by unscrupulous business leaders looking to turn a profit. They used this as an argument for staying out of international affairs. Congress passed acts declaring American neutrality in 1935 and 1936. The Neutrality Act of 1937 stated that warring nations could buy American armaments but not ammunition. The United States managed to ignore Japan's threats of expansion, even when Japanese planes sank an American gunboat in December 1937. But during his second term Roosevelt became more open to international cooperation. In his famous "quarantine" speech of 1937, he called for an agreement that would put economic pressure on aggressive nations such as Germany and Japan. Roosevelt upset isolationists in Congress and the Senate with his change of heart. But when Germany invaded France in 1940, an isolationist approach to international relations could no longer be maintained.

❖ MOB BOSSES AND BANK ROBBERS

The 1930s saw the appearance of a new kind of criminal, one who was both wealthy and powerful. The ban on alcoholic drinks during Prohibition made bootleggers (people who made and sold illegal alcohol) rich. Illegal businesses were hidden behind legitimate ones so that it became almost impossible to tell the difference. Alphonse "Al" Capone (1899–1947) was one of the most vicious and powerful of the mob leaders. He ran illegal gambling and liquor rackets and was responsible for many killings. But Capone's criminal activity was so difficult to prove that he was eventually sent to prison for nothing more than nonpayment of taxes.

In the 1930s, mob organizations operated like large corporations and had bigger ambitions than ever before. In 1929, mobsters met in Atlantic City, New Jersey, to agree on territorial boundaries. Johnny Torrio, Meyer Lansky, "Lucky" Luciano, Al Capone, and others from major cities around the country set up a commission to oversee their activities. Those who broke such agreements were dealt with violently: both Salvatore Maranzano (1868–1931) and Joe Masseria (1887–1931) were "retired" (killed) from their positions as leaders in New York in 1931 for doing so. By 1933, Lansky (1902–1983) was negotiating on a world political stage; he cut a deal with dictator Fulgencio Batista of Cuba to take control of gambling there. The U.S. government was unable to deal with the scale of the mobsters' operations. Even so, Thomas E. Dewey's (1902–1971) investigations did have some effect on exposing links between politicians and mobsters in Boston and Kansas City. Mobster "Dutch" Schultz (1902–1935) drew attention to the crime syndicate by publicly threatening to kill Dewey and was murdered as a result. On June 7, 1936, "Lucky" Luciano (1897–1962), whose gunmen had killed Schultz, was convicted on sixty-two counts of prostitution and extortion and sent to prison for between thirty and fifty years.

The great Midwestern crime wave of the 1930s made gunmen into heroes. During the Depression, outlaws were seen as outcasts and victims who were doing something to help themselves. "Pretty Boy" Floyd (1901–1934) became a latter-day Robin Hood when he burst into banks with his machine gun. Not only did he steal money, but he also took and destroyed mortgage notes, the contracts requiring people to pay off the loans on their homes. In the early 1930s, the actions of outlaws such as Clyde Barrow (1909–1934), George "Baby Face" Nelson (1908–1934), and John Dillinger (1903–1934) seemed dramatic and exciting. Hollywood

*Lucky Luciano was one of
many notorious
gangsters of the 1930s.*
*Reproduced by permission of
AP/Wide World Photos.*

picked up on the public interest in these daredevils. *The Public Enemy* (1931) shows a victimized outlaw fighting to the death against ruthless law enforcement. Hundreds of similar films were made in the early 1930s.

Although the crime sprees of individual outlaws were closely followed in the newspapers and dramatized on radio news bulletins, the American public was not sympathetic when it came to punishment. Outlaws killed lawmen and special agents. They held people captive and terrorized neighborhoods. The public would not accept such violence. In the late 1930s, gangster movies began to show more interest in the side of justice. James Cagney (1904–1986), who played a glamorous criminal in *The Public Enemy*, moved to the other side and played a special agent in *G-Men* (1935).

❖ THE FIGHT AGAINST CRIME

By 1934, the Midwestern crime wave became a national obsession. President Roosevelt (1882–1945) registered his concern in his State of the Union message that year. Attorney General Homer S. Cummings (1870–1956) came up with twelve proposals that would allow the federal government to help in a war against crime. Cummings's twelve measures are among the most important of the New Deal. They eliminated the problem of criminals escaping prosecution by crossing state lines, made it a federal offense to rob banks insured with the Deposit Insurance Corporation, and gave agents of the Bureau of Investigation (known from July 1935 as the Federal Bureau of Investigation or FBI) the authority to carry weapons and to make arrests. Despite the concern of both the president and the attorney general, it took the massacre of three police officers and one unarmed agent in Kansas City to push the measures through Congress.

*"Speakeasy" bars sold
alcohol illegally during
Prohibition. Reproduced by
permission of the
Corbis Corporation.*

One of the most famous outlaws of the 1930s was John Dillinger (1902–1934). He and his gang made a series of swift and well-organized bank robberies. Using powerful cars, safe houses, and a network of spies, Dillinger managed to evade capture for many months, making dramatic escapes from small armies of government agents. Dillinger was dubbed "public enemy number one," and the publicity of his exploits embarrassed the Bureau of Investigation. Nevertheless, FBI agents finally tracked their man, shooting and killing Dillinger on July 22, 1934.

The hunt for Dillinger did help to hone law enforcement officers' skills at catching outlaws. In the following two years they killed "Pretty Boy" Floyd, "Baby Face" Nelson, "Ma" Barker and her son Fred and arrested Alvin "Creepy" Karpis. As a result of these manhunts, the Bureau of Investigation gained its reputation as the country's top law enforcement agency.

❖ PROHIBITION

The manufacture, transportation, and sale of alcoholic drinks became illegal in the United States with the Eighteenth Amendment to the Constitution on January 16, 1920. The Volstead Act was intended to help enforce the new law. At the time, support for Prohibition was widespread. As late as 1928, Prohibition still had majority popular support. But illegal or not, many people still wanted to drink. Production of alcohol at home was restricted to illegal breweries and liquor stills, but liquor flooded across the border from Canada and was smuggled in from Europe. Bootleggers were so confident they would not be caught that they set up a pipeline to pump liquor from boats off the Jersey coast to their trucks on the shore. Illegal clubs known as "speakeasies" made alcoholic drinks available in most towns and cities. By 1930, Prohibition had given gangsters the opportunity to become rich and powerful. Attorney General William D. Mitchell (1874–1975) campaigned for more funds to catch bootleggers. But as the prisons filled up, Prohibition became less popular. By the time Franklin D. Roosevelt (1882–1945) took office in 1933, support for repeal was strong. The Twenty-first Amendment, repealing the Eighteenth, was put to the states for ratification in February 1933. On December 5 it became law. In 2001 the Eighteenth Amendment remains the only constitutional amendment to have been repealed.

For More Information

BOOKS

Barry, James P. *The Noble Experiment, 1919–1933: The Eighteenth Amendment Prohibits Liquor in America*. New York: F. Watts, 1972.

Booker, Christopher B. *African-Americans and the Presidency: A History of Broken Promises*. New York: F. Watts, 2000.

Brinkley, Alan. *Voices of Protest: Huey Long, Father Coughlin, and the Great Depression*. New York: Knopf, 1982.

Collier, Christopher, and James Lincoln Collier. *Progressivism, the Great Depression, and the New Deal, 1901 to 1941*. New York: Benchmark Books/Marshall Cavendish, 2001.

Cook, Chris, and David Waller, eds. *The Longman Handbook of Modern American History, 1763–1996*. Harlow: Longman, 1998.

Freedman, Russell. *Eleanor Roosevelt: A Life of Discovery*. New York: Clarion Books, 1993.

Freedman, Russell. *Franklin Delano Roosevelt*. New York: Clarion Books, 1990.

Hamilton, Sue L. *John Dillinger*. Bloomington, IN: Abdo & Daughters, 1989.

Isaacs, Sally Senzell. *America in the Time of Franklin Delano Roosevelt: The Story of Our Nation from Coast to Coast, from 1929 to 1948*. Des Plaines, IL: Heinemann Library, 2000.

Joseph, Paul. *Herbert Hoover*. Minneapolis: Abdo & Daughters, 2001.

Larsen, Rebecca. *Franklin D. Roosevelt: Man of Destiny*. New York: F. Watts, 1991.

Latham, Frank Brown. *FDR and the Supreme Court Fight, 1937: A President Tries to Reorganize the Federal Judiciary*. New York: F. Watts, 1972.

Lucas, Eileen. *The Eighteenth and Twenty-First Amendments: Alcohol, Prohibition, and Repeal*. Springfield, NJ: Enslow Publishers, 1998.

Pasachoff, Naomi E. *Frances Perkins: Champion of the New Deal*. Oxford: Oxford University Press Children's Books, 2000.

Polikoff, Barbara Garland. *Herbert C. Hoover, 31st President of the United States*. Ada, OK: Garrett Educational Corp., 1990.

Sifakis, Carl. *The Encyclopedia of American Crime*, 2nd ed. New York: Facts on File, 2001.

Stockdale, Tom. *The Life and Times of Al Capone*. Philadelphia, PA: Chelsea House Publishers, 1997.

Stone, Lee Tanya. *The Great Depression and World War II*. Austin, TX: Raintree Steck-Vaughn, 2001.

Woog, Adam. *Gangsters*. San Diego, CA: Lucent Books, 2000.

Woog, Adam. *Roosevelt and the New Deal*. San Diego, CA: Lucent Books, 1998.

WEB SITES

Herbert Hoover Presidential Library. http://hoover.nara.gov/ (accessed July 23, 2002).

Inaugural Addresses of the Presidents of the United States: Franklin D. Roosevelt, First Inaugural Address, March 4, 1933. http://www.bartleby.com/124/pres49.html (accessed July 23, 2002).

New Deal Network. http://newdeal.feri.org/ (accessed July 23, 2002).

Spartacus Encyclopedia of USA History. http://www.spartacus.schoolnet.co.uk/USA.htm (accessed July 23, 2002).

Lifestyles and
Social Trends

1930: Responding to the Depression, the eveningwear collections of French fashion designers include simple, low-cost cotton fabrics for the first time.

1930: Ford sells 1.15 million of its popular Model A cars.

1930: May The first airline stewardesses take to the skies with United Airlines. Job applicants had to be single women over the age of twenty-one, under five feet four inches tall, and weighing no more than 115 pounds.

1931: Lutheran churches across the country merge to form the American Lutheran Church. Congregationalists merge to form the General Council of Congregational and Christian Churches.

1931: The International Bible Students Association becomes the Jehovah's Witnesses.

1931: Nevada legalizes gambling and allows divorce for couples who have been resident in the state for only six weeks.

1931: Jane Addams wins the Nobel Peace Prize for her work with immigrants and the homeless.

1931: Schick Dry Shaver Inc. puts the world's first electric shaver on the market at $25 apiece.

1932: Henry-Russell Hitchcock and Russell Johnson introduce modern architecture to America in an exhibition at the Museum of Modern Art in New York.

1932: March 31 Ford introduces its new V8 engine in the same year as its workforce reaches a low of 46,282. In 1929, the company had employed more than 170,000 workers.

1932: May 1 The *Catholic Worker* magazine goes on sale for one cent a copy. By 1935 its circulation reaches 150,000 copies.

1933: May 27 The Century of Progress World's Fair opens on Chicago's South Side.

1933: June 6 In Camden, New Jersey, Richard M. Hollingshead Jr. opens the first drive-in movie theater.

1933: November 30 First Lady Eleanor Roosevelt sets up the White House Conference on the Emergency Needs of Women.

1934: In Germany, Adolf Hitler announces his intention to make his country as motorized as the United States.

1934: With the end of Prohibition (a ban on the sale and distribution of alcoholic beverages), sales of Coca Cola fall steadily.

1934: May 28 The Dionne quintuplets are born. Theirs is the first recorded birth of live quintuplets in the world.

1935: One in every four American households receives some form of government assistance.

1935: **April** Forty thousand visitors attend an exhibition in New York's Rockefeller Center of architect Frank Lloyd Wright's plan for urban architecture, Broadacre City.

1935: **June 10** Alcoholics Anonymous (AA) holds its first meeting in a New York hotel. The name of one of its founders, Bill Wilson, is not discovered until his death in 1971.

1935: **November 22** The first trans-Pacific air and mail service begins, flying from Alameda, California, to the Philippines. The *China Clipper* flying boat makes the first scheduled trip.

1936: Frank Lloyd Wright's Johnson Wax Building is designed in the style of "Streamline Moderne."

1936: The San Francisco Bay Bridge is completed.

1936: Six hundred thousand acres of land become part of state parks.

1936: Run-proof mascara is invented.

1937: Designer Muriel King introduces her work to the nation when she dresses Katharine Hepburn and Ginger Rogers in the movie *Stage Door*.

1937: Wallace Carothers of Du Pont invents nylon.

1937: **March 26** William H. Hastie becomes the first African American federal judge.

1937: **July 2** Famed aviator Amelia Earhart disappears on a solo flight from New Guinea to Howland Island.

1937: **August 2** The sale and possession of marijuana is outlawed by the Marijuana Traffic Act.

1938: Chemical giant Du Pont reveals its new synthetic fabrics, including rayon, a synthetic silk, and nylon.

1938: **July 3** President Franklin D. Roosevelt lights the eternal light to dedicate the Gettysburg Memorial.

1938: **July 30** Adolf Hitler's Nazi government awards Henry Ford the Grand Cross of the Supreme Order of the German Eagle, the highest award available for foreigners.

1938: **September 21** Some 63,000 people are made homeless and 680 are killed when a hurricane comes ashore across Long Island and southern New England.

1939: President Roosevelt moves Thanksgiving from the last Thursday in November to the fourth Thursday. The idea is to make the Christmas shopping period longer.

1939: **February** The Golden Gate World's Fair opens on a man-made island off San Francisco at a cost of more than $40 million dollars.

✳ *Overview*

After the stock market crash of October 29, 1929, started the Great Depression of the 1930s, Americans cut back their spending on clothes, household items, and cars. Instead of seasonal changes of wardrobe, consumers bought clothes that could be worn for years. Old cars were patched up and kept running, while the used car market expanded. From clothing and automobiles to architecture and interior design, the aim was to "use it up, wear it out, make it do, or go without."

Although the 1930s began with consumers cutting back, the decade also saw a revolution in design. Everywhere the emphasis was on efficiency. Cars, trains, and airplanes were "streamlined," allowing them to cut through the air more easily. But the idea of "Streamline Moderne," as it was called, was also applied to radios, toasters, and even buildings. By the mid-1930s the elaborate patterns and ornament of Art Deco were out. Sleek lines and simple, rounded curves were in.

In clothing, too, efficiency and simplicity were key words. Americans began to buy low-cost copies of French fashions, or they made their own. In the late 1930s, this simplicity would emerge as a distinctively American style. Everyday clothes became simpler and more versatile. Dresses were designed to be worn with accessories. This made each dress suitable for more than one occasion and was an important way of saving money. Influences on the style of men's clothes ranged from Hollywood to the British royal family.

The Depression changed the way Americans lived their lives. Many had to get used to unemployment or low pay. In 1931, ninety-five people died from malnutrition in New York City. Farmers left their land and searched for work in the cities. In the early 1930s charities in the cities had to help the starving and homeless, many of them newly arrived from rural areas. But charities themselves were short of money. The New Deal (a set of government programs designed to ease the problems caused by the Depression) stepped in to provide federal help for the poor and homeless. The misery of the Depression was lifted for some by the movies, bingo nights, chain letters, and the Irish Sweepstakes. The board game Monopoly was a huge success in the 1930s.

Immigrants who arrived in the United States in the 1920s depended on charities, loan companies, and the banks. After 1929, many lost their entire means of support. For African Americans, the situation was also very bad. Many lost their jobs when employers decided to employ white workers instead. Many tenant farmers and sharecroppers (farmers who worked plots of land that they rented) lost their land and source of income. Unemployment for black workers was 48 percent in 1932. For the United States as a whole it was 25 percent.

As the Depression deepened, attendance at church declined. Many of the poor were ashamed of their new status. Others turned away in despair. The churches where numbers rose tended to be conservative in outlook, such as the Pentecostal and the Southern Baptist churches. Religion also took a political turn, with Jews and Roman Catholics siding with the Democrats and President Roosevelt's New Deal programs, and Protestants with the Republicans. Only African Americans bucked the trend. Black Protestants were nearly all in favor of the New Deal.

James Cannon Jr. (1864–1944) James Cannon Jr., a bishop of the Methodist Episcopal Church, was one of the strongest proponents of Prohibition and a leader of the Anti-Saloon League, a group that campaigned against alcohol consumption. In the 1928 presidential election, he organized opposition to Alfred E. Smith (1873–1944), the Roman Catholic opponent to Herbert Hoover (1874–1964). Cannon was one of the most influential church leaders of the 1930s. His career was finally wrecked by a series of scandals. Although found not guilty in 1934 of stealing election money, he was forced into retirement. *Photo courtesy of the Library of Congress.*

Hattie Carnegie (1889–1956) Born in Vienna, Hattie Carnegie became one of New York's most celebrated dress designers of the 1930s. She began her career as a milliner, making hats, but made her name adapting French dress styles for American tastes. She believed clothes should be simple. If a dress is too often admired, she said, be suspicious of it. Clothes should "enhance the charm of the woman who wears them." In addition to creating her own designs, Carnegie trained many of the American designers of the younger generation. *Photo reproduced by permission of the Corbis Corporation.*

Mary Williams Dewson (1874–1962) Known to her friends as Molly, Mary Williams Dewson studied history at Wellesley College. Her class predicted she would be president of the United States. After graduating, Dewson campaigned for women's rights, the rights of women prisoners, and for the minimum wage. She was influential in the first Roosevelt administration in various leadership positions in the Democratic National Committee and the Social Security Board, and she helped many women to positions in government. She retired because of ill health in 1938, although she remained active in politics at a lower level for the rest of her life.

W. E. B. Du Bois (1868–1963) In 1895, W.E.B. Du Bois became the first black student to be awarded a Ph.D. from Harvard University. From this beginning he spent much of his life researching and writing about the black community. In his best-known work, *The Souls of Black Folks* (1903), he describes the difficulty of feeling both black and American. Du Bois eventually turned to direct action. He was a founder of the National Association for the Advancement of Colored People (NAACP) and is considered the father of the black civil rights movement. *Photo courtesy of the Library of Congress.*

Valentina (1904–1989) Born in Kiev, Ukraine, Valentina considered herself an architect of dresses. She relocated to New York City from Athens, Greece, in 1923, and her inspiration came from classical Greek architecture. Working with her husband she produced expensive dresses for wealthy customers. She was always determined to make dresses that fitted the customer perfectly in terms of both cut and appearance. Valentina also made stage and movie costumes for such stars as Greta Garbo (1905–1990) and was famous for using hoods, fur hats, and scarf handkerchiefs in her designs.

Stephen Samuel Wise (1874–1949) In 1907, Stephen Samuel Wise founded the Free Synagogue of New York. He spent the rest of his career there as a leading rabbi in Reform Judaism. He argued for Zionism, the return of Jews to Palestine, and tried to organize an opposition movement to the Nazis in 1933. His plan to withdraw the United States from the 1936 Berlin Olympics failed. Jewish immigration to the United States increased in the 1930s. But more significant was the movement of Jews from Europe into Palestine. Wise supported this movement even though it created an antiSemitic backlash in the United States.

Frank Lloyd Wright (1867–1959) America's most famous architect, Frank Lloyd Wright had a career that spanned seventy years. He pioneered the use of concrete blocks in building, but he also tried to make his buildings blend well with their environment. Open plan interiors are one of his trademark styles. His mature career began with the Prairie Style, a revival of the architecture of the Great Plains. Wright worked on some of the most important buildings of the twentieth century, including the Imperial Hotel (1922) in Tokyo, Fallingwater (1936) in Mill Run, Pennsylvania, and the Johnson Wax building (1939) in Racine, Wisconsin. *Photo reproduced by permission of the Corbis Corporation.*

◆◆ *Topics in the News* . . . .

❖ AMERICA'S LOVE AFFAIR WITH THE AUTOMOBILE CONTINUES DESPITE HARD TIMES

By the 1930s the automobile had become a symbol of wealth, convenience, and leisure. Even when times were hard, Americans were reluctant to give up their cars. In the 1920s, the auto industry had encouraged consumers to buy a new car rather than repair an old one. Finance deals spread the cost over three years, which was the time it took for a new model to come out. But renewing model ranges so frequently was expensive for manufacturers. By the late 1920s the market for used cars was flooded with cheap, reliable vehicles. During the Depression, Americans who purchased cars bought these used models, which reduced the volume of new car sales.

Auto executive Alfred P. Sloan (1875–1966) brought General Motors (GM) through the Depression ahead of its main rivals, Ford and Chrysler. He did so by creating a "car for every purse and purpose" and by constantly upgrading each model. Sloan's strategy, known as "Sloanism," encouraged consumers to trade up when the time came to change their vehicle. He also allowed consumers to trade in their old cars, so that GM, rather than an outside dealer, could sell the used vehicles. Under Sloan's management, GM also introduced the idea of automobiles created by designers rather than engineers. It was an important innovation in the auto industry.

Before the 1930s, automobiles were box-shaped, with their separate elements—fenders, passenger compartment, running board, and trunk—clearly visible. The Styling Section at GM designed automobiles that were more of "one piece." The 1932 Cadillac brought the trunk into the body of the car, while the 1933 Chevrolet hid the radiator behind a grille. In 1938, Cadillac did away with the running board below the doors. This made it possible to widen the body and give more room inside. Cars lost their box shape and began to take on a sleek, curved profile. There were many advantages to streamlining. It increased interior space and produced less wind drag. Streamlined cars were quieter, faster, and more fuel efficient.

Going on sale in 1934, the Chrysler and DeSoto Airflow was one of the most remarkable automobiles of the 1930s. It sold fewer than eleven thousand units in three years of production, but it was one of the most aerodynamic cars of its day. It was the first car to have the chassis, or frame, built into its body. This made it lighter and more stable. At the Chicago Century of Progress Exhibition in 1933, a prototype Airflow sedan stood next to the Union Pacific M-1000 Streamliner train.

The V8 engine Ford introduced in 1932 set the standard for American engine design. With its eight cylinders arranged in a "V" formation when viewed from the front, the V8 became a feature of classic American cars for years to come. In 1932, its extra power was greatly appreciated. Bank robber John Dillinger (1903–1934) wrote Ford to say: "I can make any other car take a Ford's dust." Outlaw Clyde Barrow (1909–1934) was also impressed. He wrote: "Even if my business hasn't been strictly legal it don't hurt anything to tell you what a fine car you got in the V8." Ford's 1932 model also lowered the body in between the wheels to give the car greater stability.

❖ **ARCHITECTS DEVELOP NEW STYLES**

Art deco was a trend in architecture and design that began in Europe. Using rich, heavyweight materials such as marble, wood veneer, and stainless steel, art deco designers and architects decorated entrance portals, elevator lobbies, and corridors with geometric patterns and swooping curves. Art deco reached its peak in the United States with the Chrysler Building, built in 1930. By the early 1930s, however, art deco was being replaced

The DeSoto sedan was a popular automobile during the 1930s.
Reproduced by permission of the American Automobile Association.

with simpler designs based on structure and form rather than ornamentation. One of these new styles was known as functionalism. Beginning in Moscow just after World War I, the idea of functionalism was to think of buildings as if they were machines. If the building did its job well, it was considered beautiful.

Like the functionalists, Walter Gropius (1883–1969), founder of the Bauhaus design school in Germany, was also influenced by the machine age. But Gropius believed that architects should be artists as well as engineers. His approach combined technology with the human elements of arts and crafts. Bauhaus-designed buildings celebrated community life and encouraged people to socialize in public spaces. Gropius immigrated to America in 1937 and became head of the Harvard University School of Architecture. From there his ideas influenced a generation of American architects.

Like Walter Gropius, American architect Frank Lloyd Wright (1867–1959) was interested in building high-quality, low-cost housing. But unlike the Bauhaus founder, Wright drew on nature, rather than machines, for his inspiration. Wright used the idea of building in sympathy with the environment in many of his projects. The best known of these is Fallingwater (1936). Built over a waterfall in Mill Run, Pennsylvania, Fallingwater is one of the most important buildings of the twentieth century. The rocks of the waterfall are part of the house. Many of the walls are glass, opening out on concrete porches. The whole building is surrounded by trees.

❖ AMERICAN BUILDINGS, FROM SKYSCRAPERS TO DRIVE-INS

Two buildings in New York City offered hope for the future: The Chrysler Building (1930) and the Empire State Building (1931) were the two tallest buildings in the world. Designed by William Van Alen (1883–1954), the Chrysler Building was inspired by machines and streamlining. Its stainless steel pinnacle makes it one of the most recognizable buildings in the world. The Empire State Building opened on May

Day 1931, and was the tallest building in the world until the World Trade Center overtook it forty years later. The opening of the Empire State Building was attended by governor of New York Franklin D. Roosevelt (1882–1945) and Mayor Jimmy Walker (1881–1946). In an action considered by some as symbolic of his "hands off" presidency, Herbert Hoover (1874–1964) pretended to throw a switch in Washington to turn on the lights in the building.

Planned as a skyscraper city on Manhattan Island, the Rockefeller Center was built as an arts center, commercial area, and a new theater for the Metropolitan Opera. John D. Rockefeller Jr. (1874–1960), one of the richest men in the United States, was its chief supporter. After the 1929 stock market crash, the Metropolitan Opera pulled out, leaving Rockefeller to do as he wished. He built residential buildings, office space, a mall, and what has become a famous ice rink. The original thirteen buildings were built between 1932 and 1940. The 70-story RCA building and the Radio City Music Hall are among the best known. The public gardens, sculptures, ice rink, and murals are in keeping with the original idea of the center as a public space.

President Franklin D. Roosevelt (1882–1945) used government money to erect buildings and stimulate the economy. The creation of the Public Works Administration (PWA) in 1932 released $3.3 billion to build roads, bridges, and public buildings. Another New Deal agency, the Works Progress Administration (WPA), also funded buildings, from the San Francisco–Oakland Bay Bridge (1934) to the U.S. Supreme Court building in Washington, D.C. (1935).

Something new in American architecture could also be seen along roadsides from coast to coast. In the poverty-stricken 1930s, Americans on vacation, and searching for work, took to the road. Tourist camps, diners, and camping sites sprang up everywhere. To attract the attention of passing drivers, oversized animals, such as the Big Duck in Riverhead, Long Island, were built by the roadside. American roads were transformed by Chinese pagodas, Dutch windmills, and Native American-style teepees. The famous Brown Derby restaurant in Hollywood, California, was built in the shape of a brown derby hat.

OPPOSITE PAGE
The Empire State Building, designed by William Van Alen, was built in 1931. Reproduced by permission of Archive Photos, Inc.

❖ FALLING CHURCH ATTENDANCE AND SHIFTING RELIGIOUS LOYALTIES

Despite the hardship of the Depression, Americans did not turn to religion for comfort. In fact, church attendance declined in the 1930s. This was partly because people were embarrassed when they were unem-

Religion and the Depression

Most churches were involved in charity work during the Depression. While some were intolerant of the poor and unemployed, claiming they brought hardship on themselves, this was not true in all cases, even among white Protestant denominations that had traditionally supported conservative Republican values and traditions. The Methodist Episcopal Church was one of the most outspoken critics of President Hoover's economic policies. In 1932 it produced a report stating that capitalism was sinful because it tolerated poverty. "Private ownership," the report went on, "has failed to keep industry functioning." Some feared that the Methodist Episcopal Church had gone socialist.

ployed and partly because people moved around more and lost the "habit" of going to church. Understandably, contributions to churches also fell, leaving many churches in debt.

Religious communities were divided along political lines. While most African Americans voted Democratic, white Protestants were mostly Republican. White Roman Catholics supported Democratic New Deal programs. Herbert Hoover's 1928 presidential election victory over Catholic Alfred E. Smith (1873–1944) was reassuring for conservative Protestants. But the times were changing. The fastest growing Protestant groups, including the Pentecostals and Southern Baptists, were small, fundamentalist groups. The major religions were in decline. In the 1930s, Protestant dominance began to give way to a more diverse, more democratic religious influence.

Jews formed the third major religious group in the United States in the 1930s. They were divided between Reform, Conservative, and Orthodox communities, and between German and Eastern European origins. The question of whether American Jews should support the Jewish settlement of Palestine was a major issue. With the Holocaust still an unimaginable nightmare, many American Jews feared that Jewish immigration would trigger anti-Semitism (hatred toward Jews) among Christian Americans. However, as German leader Adolf Hitler's extermination program began to gather pace in Germany, European Jews fled to the United States anyway.

One way Americans managed to get the look of expensive Paris fashions without paying the high prices was bootlegging. In 1936, buyers from major American department stores attended the Paris fashion shows. They bought hundreds of dresses and brought them back to the United States. But instead of selling them, they had copies made. American stores sold perfect copies of dresses by Chanel and Vionnet for about $100—one fifth of the cost of the originals. The stores also took advantage of export laws. If they returned the original dresses to France within six months, they paid very little import duty. Once the dresses had been copied, the originals went on sale in the backstreets of Paris.

❖ A NEW LOOK IN AMERICAN FASHION

When the Depression hit, Americans had less money to spend on clothes. There was also a change of mood. So-called "flappers" had celebrated the "roaring twenties" wearing waistless, narrow dresses. They wore them with long strings of jewelry and elaborate shawls and hats. The flapper disappeared almost overnight at the beginning of the 1930s. For ordinary Americans clothing became more mature, more elegant, and more reasonably priced. The emphasis shifted to clothes that were versatile and practical.

The 1930s saw a change in the kinds of fabrics used in American clothes as well. Simple cotton fabrics such as organdy, piqué, and lace made a comeback, even for eveningwear. Expensive embroidery, beads, and delicate silks all but disappeared. New materials took their place. A stretchy material called "Lastex" was used in swimwear and skiwear. With money in short supply, most women no longer changed their wardrobe with each new season. Instead they bought new hats, gloves, pocketbooks, shoes, and jewelry to freshen up dresses they already owned.

By 1930 Paris had dominated American fashion for more than a century. But in the Depression, American designers began to take over. They produced high-quality, fashionable clothes. Mollie Parnis (1902–1992) was among the first American designers to be known to the public by name. But at between $79 and $195 for a single dress, her clothes were not cheap. American fashion became known for its sporty, relaxed style in the

The Look for Women

For most American women, the dominant fashion of the 1930s was the print dress. Often made from new synthetic materials, the print dress usually had a belted waist and a slightly flared, below-the-knee skirt. Unlike the narrow, tubular dresses of the 1920s, the print dress emphasized the waistline and bloused loosely in the top. Sleeves were mid-length, while shoes were low-heeled and more comfortable than before.

1930s. Designers such as Clare Potter (1903–1999) made it acceptable to wear sportswear on the street. Muriel King (1900–1977), who designed for Lord and Taylor, made clothes that were worn by everyone, from the average American woman to glamorous movie stars. But the most famous American designer of the 1930s was Elizabeth Hawes (1903–1971). After achieving success showing her work in Paris, in 1932 she designed a ready-made coat and dress that sold for $10.75. The twenty-five dresses she showed in Paris each sold for ten times that amount.

One of the reasons for the success of American fashion in the 1930s was Hollywood. In the 1930s, Hollywood needed costumes that looked good in black and white. Dressing men this way was easy. But for women's costumes, the film industry had to steer away from the trend for patterned prints. Dressed by Adrian (1903–1959), stars such as Joan Crawford, Greta Garbo, and Marlene Dietrich had a major influence on popular tastes. Clothes stores quickly followed the styles as they appeared in popular movies.

Not all Americans joined in the move toward austerity in fashion and social life, however. Among the very wealthy in America's major cities, December was the month when families "introduced" their sixteen- and seventeen-year-old daughters into society. The young girls were known as "debutantes" or "debs" because this was their debut social "season." Despite the Depression, families like the Kennedys in Boston and the Vanderbilts in New York spent freely on lavish balls. Debs went to a different dance or social event almost every night from November to January. For these events debs wore expensive dresses and jewelry, often imported from Paris. Magazines such as *Life* and the *Saturday Evening Post* published photographs of these events.

The Look for Men

As in the 1920s, men's suits emphasized the chest. Jackets were high waisted with wide, short lapels. Trousers were wide and long in the leg. Heavy shoes balanced the loose trousers. Men's fashion was heavily influenced by movie stars such as Clark Gable (1901–1960). But perhaps the strongest single influence came from Britain. The Prince of Wales introduced the double-breasted dinner jacket, the "Windsor" necktie knot, and the backless waistcoat. By the end of the decade, hat brims were wider, jacket shoulders were heavily padded, and trousers were straighter. The zipper replaced buttons in the fly.

❖ FAMILIES STRUGGLE IN A FAILING ECONOMY

In 1935 it was estimated that the average-sized American family needed $2,000 per year to maintain a comfortable lifestyle. Unfortunately, the average household income was only half that. Families had to cut back on expenses such as new cars and household goods. It was mostly women who managed the household budgets. They began making their own clothes and food. Radio shows and magazines gave tips for saving money, while sales of glass jars, used for pickling and preserving, went up. Sales of ready-made goods fell. When the economy improved later in the decade women slowed down on their baking and mending and went back to being consumers.

While women found themselves working harder in the home, men had different problems to face. Most men saw their role as being to provide for their families. Unemployment was thus a humiliating and frightening ordeal. When they lost their jobs, many men became depressed. Suicides became more common, while many others deserted their wives and families without warning.

In the early 1930s, the high cost of marrying, setting up home, and having children led many couples to avoid or postpone marriage. Divorces were also expensive, so the divorce rate fell too. But the general drop in divorce rates did not mean marriages were happier. As the Depression dragged on into 1933 and beyond, many families did eventually fall apart under the strain. The number of married couples living apart reached 1.5 million in 1940. By 1940, divorce rates were back to 1920s levels.

By 1933, for the first time in U.S. history, the number of births fell below the number needed to replace the population. For many couples, the chance to marry passed them by. Weddings were cancelled or postponed due to lack of money or the need to travel in search of work. Engagements grew longer, and premarital sex became much more common. Many longstanding couples broke up before marrying, but most survived long engagements to marry in the late 1930s.

Despite the pressures of a poor economy, not all families were unhappy. Many families found that the Depression brought them closer together. Women took part-time jobs, while children earned pocket money delivering newspapers, shining shoes, and mowing lawns. Many elderly people moved in with their grown children, and relatives helped one another to get by. Families entertained themselves at home more than before. They played cards, checkers, and the popular new board game, Monopoly. But while this arrangement was cozy for some, for others it was restricting and unpleasant. There was very little privacy. When cheap housing began to appear in the 1940s, most of these large family groups broke up.

❖ AMERICANS AND INDIVIDUALISM

The idea of American individualism goes back to the founding fathers. It held that Americans should be independent and self-reliant, not depending on the government or other groups but only on their own hard work. But in the 1930s this idea of a nation of individuals was seriously challenged. When unemployment and poverty struck, many people found that they depended on others to survive. Americans began to see themselves as members of communities and interest groups, rather than isolated individuals. This change in attitude led directly to the major political changes of the 1930s. From the rise of the labor unions to the Social Security Act (in which the government provided money for people in old age), American politics reflected a growing sense of the nation as a community working together.

Despite the growing enthusiasm for collective action and trade unions, fewer than 100,000 Americans belonged to the socialist or communist parties of the 1930s. (Both parties rejected individualism and capitalism in favor of government or society-wide responsibility for the economy.) Even so, some historians have labeled the 1930s the "red decade." Initially, many communists objected to the New Deal because they thought it would end democracy and lead to fascism. But they soon realized that criticism of the New Deal might split the political left. Realizing that New Deal policies had a lot of support from voters, socialists and communists quickly joined the "popular front" against the conservatives.

A 1937 study discovered that American college students ran a competitive system of measuring popularity. The highest scores were achieved by wearing the "right" clothes, owning a car, and being seen with the "right" people. For women, a high score depended on being seen with the right men and by playing hard to get. If she did well, a young woman could create an image of being "special." At the University of Michigan, men who conformed to the "dating standard" were awarded the title "Big Man on Campus" (BMOC) by sorority women.

Progressive reformers such as Jane Addams (1860–1945) and Florence Kelly (1859–1932) had argued for years that society depended on people working together. Even self-supporting farmers relied on factory workers to provide them with machinery and tools. Progressive New Dealers put their dream of a more supportive, community-based society into action through legislation such as the Social Security Act of 1935. Conservatives opposing the New Deal argued that individual effort was needed to rescue the nation from economic ruin. But the pronouncements of conservatives such as Albert Lasker (1880–1952) only made Americans even more committed to the New Deal. While left-wing progressives were accused of being "reds," conservatives were blamed for the disastrous economic politics of the 1920s.

❖ THRILLS SMALL AND LARGE

Local fairs had long been a part of American life. In rural areas they involved showing prize livestock and produce. Sporting competitions and rodeos were often featured, as were such competitions as guessing the weight of the pumpkin, and prizes for the best-tasting cake. Many fairs celebrated a famous historical event, but most were just an excuse for an annual community jamboree. By the 1930s they included displays of parachuting or wing walking, where somebody would stand on the wing of a flying plane. Elaborate carnival rides traveled from one fair to the next. During the Depression, local fairs were a welcome form of cheap amusement.

While small-scale fairs were common across the country, World's Fairs took place in major cities. They were built on a large scale, lasted for many months, and cost millions of dollars. In many cases, World's Fairs were an attempt to boost the economy of the host city. The exhibits were forward-looking and optimistic. Corporations used World's Fairs to show off their products, while the fair site often included permanent new buildings. Many people thought that spending money on World's Fairs could help to put an end to the Depression.

Chicago held its Century of Progress Exhibition in 1933 to 1934. Planning began late in the 1920s, but the exhibition was designed to boost the city's economy. Its theme of scientific and technological progress was a reminder that the Depression would not last forever. Exhibits included a working oil refinery, a Ford assembly plant, and a radio-controlled tractor. Entertainments included the Sky-Ride, shuttling visitors around the exhibition grounds on a rail suspended two hundred feet in the air. An "odditorium" included a theater troupe made up of sixty midgets, and Sally Rand (1904–1979), who performed a nude "fan dance." Attendance at the fair was 22.5 million in 1933 and 16.4 million in 1934. Still it managed to make only a small profit.

The Golden Gate International Exposition was held in 1939 and 1940. It was hoped that the fair would provide work for the unemployed and generate income from tourists. A four hundred-acre island was built in San Francisco Bay. Known as Treasure Island, it was reached by ferry, or by a road link to Yerba Buena Island. Like Chicago's fair, the Golden Gate Exposition featured fantastic architecture and exhibitions from corporations. There were also amusements such as ferris wheels and a roller coaster. Sally Rand made another appearance, this time with her "Nude Ranch" show. Yet even with this visual feast to attract visitors, the fair closed with a deficit of more than a half a million dollars.

With the theme of "The World of Tomorrow," the New York World's Fair (1939–1940) was the greatest of the decade. The fair was divided into nine zones: Amusements, Communications and Business Systems, Community Interests, Food, Government, Medicine and Public Health, Production and Distribution, Science and Education, and Transportation. At its center were the Trylon, a tower 610 feet high, and the Perisphere, a globe 180 feet across. Inside was displayed the "Democracity," a model of the city of the future. It was at the New York World's Fair, at the RCA exhibit, that President Roosevelt (1882–1945) made the first televised address by a U.S. president. The General Motors exhibit, created by Norman Bel Geddes (1893–1958), showed the United States as it might appear in the 1960s. In that far-off future, cars were fueled by liquid air, cancer had been cured, and everyone graduated from high school.

The New York World's Fair lost a total of $18.7 million. Yet it had managed to catch the attention of the public, generating optimism for a better future. This optimism, however, like the fair itself, was short-lived. After the closing of the Fair, the Trylon and Perisphere were broken up for scrap to help the war effort.

For More Information

BOOKS

Allen, Frederick Lewis. *Since Yesterday: The 1930s in America, September 3, 1929–September 3, 1939.* New York: HarperCollins, 1986.

Blackman, Cally. *The 20s and 30s: Flappers and Vamps.* Milwaukee, WI: Gareth Stevens, 2000.

Blum, Stella. *Everyday Fashions of the Thirties as Pictured in Sears Catalogs.* New York: Dover, 1986.

Carson, Richard Burns. *The Olympian Cars: The Great American Luxury Automobiles of the Twenties and Thirties.* New York: Knopf, 1976.

Constantino, Maria, Elane Feldman, and Valerie Cumming, editors. *Fashions of a Decade: The 1930s (Fashions of a Decade Series).* New York: Facts on File, 1992.

Cook, Chris, and David Waller, editors. *The Longman Handbook of Modern American History, 1763–1996.* New York: Longman, 1998.

Feinstein, Stephen. *The 1930s: From the Great Depression to the Wizard of Oz (Decades of the Twentieth Century).* New York: Enslow Publishers, 2001.

Harris, Cyril M. *American Architecture: An Illustrated Encyclopedia.* New York: W. W. Norton, 1998.

Hawes, Elizabeth. *Fashion Is Spinach.* New York: Random House, 1938.

Hunt, Marsha. *The Way We Wore: Styles of the 1930s and '40s and Our World Since Then.* Fallbrook, CA: Fallbrook, 1993.

Klehr, Harvey. *The Heyday of American Communism: The Depression Decade.* New York: Basic Books, 1984.

Lucas, Eileen. *The Eighteenth and Twenty-first Amendments: Alcohol, Prohibition, and Repeal.* Springfield, NJ: Enslow Publishers, 1998.

Margolies, John. *Fun Along the Road: American Tourist Attractions.* Boston: Little, Brown, 1998.

Martin, Richard. *Jocks and Nerds: Men's Style in the Twentieth Century.* New York: Rizzoli, 1989.

Melton, J. Gordon. *American Religions: An Illustrated History.* Santa Barbara, CA: ABC-CLIO, 2000.

Moloney, James H. *Encyclopedia of American Cars, 1930–1942.* Glen Ellyn, IL: Crestline, 1977.

Nishi, Dennis. *Life During the Great Depression*. San Diego, CA: Lucent Books, 1998.

Press, Petra. *The 1930s (Cultural History of the United States Through the Decades)*. San Diego: Lucent, 1999.

Roesch, Roberta. *World's Fairs: Yesterday, Today, Tomorrow*. New York: John Day, 1964.

Terkel, Studs. *Hard Times: An Oral History of the Great Depression*. New York: Random House, 1970.

Vlack, Don. *Art Deco Architecture in New York, 1920–1940*. New York: Harper and Rowe, 1974.

PERIODICALS

"Eastern Methodists Go Socialist." *Christian Century* 49 (April 13, 1932): pp. 467.

WEB SITES

American Architecture—Twentieth Century—1930 to 1939. http://www. greatbuildings.com/types/usa/usa_1930–1939.html (accessed July 23, 2002).

The Costume Gallery: Women's Fashions 1930s. http://www.costumegallery.com/ 1930.htm (accessed July 23, 2002).

Frank Lloyd Wright Foundation. http://www.franklloydwright.org/ (accessed July 23, 2002).

Industrial Designers and Streamlining. http://www.pbs.org/wgbh/amex/ streamliners/peopleevents/p_designers.html (accessed July 23, 2002).

chapter six *Medicine and Health*

1930: Karl Landsteiner wins the Nobel Prize for his work in identifying and understanding the interrelationship of the blood groups A, B, AB, and O.

1930: The common cold virus is discovered.

1930: X ray becomes more widely used. It is used to examine a range of ailments, from brain tumors to problems with the spleen.

1930: September The *American Journal of the Diseases of Childhood* recommends vitamin D as a protection against tooth decay. Antiseptic mouth washes, the article goes on, are of no benefit.

1931: A polio epidemic brings the disease to public attention. At around the same time, scientists manage to grow the virus in the laboratory, taking the first step toward a vaccine.

1931: The number of deaths from appendicitis continues to rise.

1931: January Rheumatoid arthritis is discovered to be caused by an infection.

1931: March 20 U.S. Federal Council of Churches approves the limited use of birth control methods.

1932: The Benzedrine Inhaler is invented and used as a spray to clear nasal congestion.

1932: At Northwestern University School of Medicine, scientists cure stomach ulcers using the mucus membrane from pigs' stomachs. The mucus is put in ice cream and fruit juices and eaten by patients.

1932: A serum is developed to treat yellow fever.

1932: April 4 Vitamin C is identified.

1933: T. H. Morgan wins the Nobel Prize for medicine for his work on genetics.

1933: The Blue Cross hospital insurance program is started.

1933: April 5 The first operation to remove a cancerous lung is performed.

1933: November 4 The drug aphadinitrophenol is used to treat obesity. It works by speeding up the patient's metabolism, but can be fatal in large doses.

1933: December 11 Transplant surgery moves closer when parts of the thyroid and parathyroid gland are transferred from one patient to another.

1933: December 21 Dried human blood serum is developed.

1934: A Nobel Prize goes to George Hoyt Whipple, George Minot, and William P. Murphy for their therapy for anemia.

1934: Evipan, an anesthetic from Germany, is first used in the United States at the George Washington University Medical School.

1934: Liver extract cures the fatal blood disease agranulocytosis.

1935: The first hospital for drug addicts is opened in Lexington, Kentucky.

1935: The public becomes skeptical about human vaccination when trials of a polio vaccine go wrong and several children contract the disease from the vaccine; one dies.

1935: Scientists at Yale find that when they remove the front part of the brains of monkeys, the animals become much calmer. The procedure, known as bilateral prefrontal lobotomy, is later used to treat violent psychiatric patients.

1935: June 10 Alcoholics Anonymous is founded in New York.

1935: June 20 The first mechanical heart keeps organs alive outside the body.

1936: "Sulfa" drugs are introduced to the United States. They help treat various infectious diseases.

1936: The Federal Children's Bureau reports that infant deaths are falling. But the number of mothers dying in childbirth is still high, at fifty-nine of every ten thousand live births.

1936: At the Rockefeller Institute, the polio virus is grown in human brain cells.

1937: The first evidence of a link between cigarette smoking and lung cancer is observed.

1937: The National Cancer Institute is established.

1937: An elixir of sulfanimide, used to treat bacterial infections, kills many children.

1937: March 15 The first modern blood bank is set up at Cook County Hospital, Chicago.

1937: August A study from the Federal Children's Bureau shows that 86 out of every 1,000 black children born do not survive. For white children, the figure is 53 per 1,000.

1937: September 23 The National Foundation for Infantile Paralysis is founded by Franklin D. Roosevelt in Warm Springs, Georgia.

1938: Birth control is legal, except in Connecticut, Mississippi, and Massachusetts.

1938: February 24 The first toothbrushes with nylon bristles go on sale in New Jersey.

1938: April 12 New York becomes the first state requiring couples to have a medical examination before marrying.

1939: New research leads to the revival of research into penicillin. This marks the start of widespread use of antibiotics to treat bacterial infections.

Overview

Major developments in the field of medicine and health occurred during the 1930s. Scientists developed vaccines for crippling diseases like poliomyelitis (commonly known as polio), while new "sulfa" drugs promised therapy for a wide range of infections. New anesthetics made surgery safer and less painful. What stood in the way of dramatic improvements in public health was the Depression. By the mid-1930s, the average national income in the United States was half that of 1929. With nearly 40 percent of some states' populations on government relief, fewer patients could afford to pay for medical care. Physicians earned less as a result, but many continued to treat charity cases for free. Hospitals had similar problems. In the absence of modern drug therapies, the average hospital stay in 1933 was two weeks. Many patients could not afford to pay, so beds remained empty while people suffered at home.

Large increases in deaths from cancer, respiratory diseases, and heart attacks occurred during the Depression. Syphilis, a sexually transmitted disease, affected as many as 10 percent of Americans, a rate higher than that in any other industrialized nation with records. The main causes of death in the early 1930s, in order of risk, were: heart disease, cancer, pneumonia, and infections and parasitic disorders. This last group included influenza (flu), tuberculosis, and syphilis.

Polio was a serious problem in the 1930s. In 1931 there was a large outbreak that spread across the Northeast. In 1932, Philadelphia was hit, and in 1934 Los Angeles was affected. The year 1939 saw outbreaks in South Carolina, Buffalo, and New York. Many Americans did not realize that their president, Franklin D. Roosevelt, had been crippled by poliomyelitis (polio) in 1921. Although he wore leg braces and moved around in a wheelchair, this was not generally reported in the news. On the rare occasions he stood at a public event, his legs were hidden from view.

Little was known about how the disease was transmitted or how it could be stopped. Vaccines were being developed, but before the Food, Drug, and Cosmetic Act was amended in 1938, vaccines did not have to be tested or licensed by the U.S. Public Health Service. It is estimated that as many as one in every thousand cases of polio in 1935 was actually caused by trials of vaccines. Such failures were a serious blow to research. In the midst of the Depression, money for research was scarce. Roosevelt used his influence to help create the March of Dimes campaign, one of America's most successful fundraisers.

Despite their difficulties in containing some diseases, scientists made great strides in understanding the body and curing disease during the decade. Karl Landsteiner won America's second Nobel Prize for medicine in 1930 for his work identifying the blood groups. Other winners in the 1930s included Thomas Hunt Morgan for research in genetics and George R. Minot, William P. Murphy, and G. H. Whipple for their work on the blood disease pernicious anemia. In 1936, five years after Austrian researchers discovered two strains of poliovirus, Albert B. Sabin managed to grow the virus in the laboratory. This would pave the way for effective vaccines in the future. Other advances included faster, cheaper X-ray machines, better blood transfusions, and the widespread use of hormones, vitamins, and insulin in therapy.

President Roosevelt's social reform program, called the New Deal, marked the first time the federal government addressed the nation's health. From plans to provide better housing to the Farm Security Administration (FSA), New Deal agencies provided medical insurance, childcare, help for the disabled, and boosts in public health campaigns. The Food, Drug, and Cosmetic Act of 1938 protected the public from quack doctors and dangerous drugs or procedures.

Although Congress debated the idea of a national health insurance program, attempts to establish one failed. Instead, voluntary health insurance became more widespread in the 1930s. First, the American Hospital Association (AHA) created the Blue Cross plan in 1933 to pay for hospital costs. Then in 1939, Blue Shield was put in place to cover other medical costs. Doctors objected to government involvement in health care, but three quarters of Americans approved of government help with paying for health care. By the 1930s the fee-for-service system of paying for medical services was not working. Reform began with the New Deal. But the issue of who should pay for health care was still being argued in the twenty-first century.

Alexis Carrel (1873–1944) Alexis Carrel immigrated to the United States from France in 1904. He was awarded the Nobel Prize for Medicine in 1912 for his work on the transplantation of blood vessels. His techniques marked the beginnings of heart surgery and organ transplants. In 1935, along with aviator Charles Lindbergh (1902–1974), Carrel built the first mechanical heart. Carrel's political views made him unpopular with his employers at the Rockefeller Center. He returned to France at the beginning of World War II, where he worked for the French Ministry of Public Health. *Photo reproduced by permission of the Corbis Corporation.*

Morris Fischbein (1889–1976) Morris Fischbein was one of the strongest opponents of regulation of the medical profession. Through the American Medical Association (AMA), Fischbein fought to stop doctors' cooperatives and corporations taking over healthcare. He disliked the fact that they paid doctors fixed salaries and used insurance schemes to pay for them. Fischbein thought that such "socialized medicine," as he called it, would turn doctors into mere laborers. As one of the most influential leaders of the AMA, Fischbein had many supporters. But by the end of the 1930s medical insurance was a popular and sensible choice for most patients.

Karen Horney (1885–1952) In 1932, Karen Horney became the assistant director at the newly opened Psychoanalytic Institute in Chicago. She argued against the ideas of the founder of psychoanalysis, Sigmund Freud (1856–1939). Where Freud thought that personality disturbance was caused by denying human instinct, Horney blamed it on the patients' upbringing. Horney's criticism of Freud left her alienated in the psychoanalytic community. She went on to found the American Institute of Psychoanalysis and had a major influence on the feminist movement of the 1960s. *Photo reproduced by permission of the Corbis Corporation.*

Karl Landsteiner (1868–1943) Karl Landsteiner became an American citizen in 1929 and won the Nobel Prize for medicine in 1930. His discovery of blood types, which are now categorized as A, B, AB, and O, made transfusions possible. Landsteiner was also interested in polio. He was the first to infect monkeys with the disease, giving other scientists a way of studying polio in the laboratory. In 1939, Landsteiner and his colleagues discovered a further blood subdivision. Each group could be Rh positive or negative. Landsteiner's work on blood and the immune system saved many lives. *Photo courtesy of the Library of Congress.*

Thomas Parran (1892–1968) Thomas Parran became surgeon general in 1936 and began his famous campaign against syphilis and sexually transmitted disease. The campaign began with an article in the *Survey Graphic* and *Reader's Digest* magazines called "Stamp Out Syphilis." Parran succeeded in redefining syphilis in the public mind as a curable illness, but he never was able to convince Americans that syphilis was a medical problem rather than a moral one. Despite one of the most famous public health campaigns in American history, syphilis was still a major killer at the end of the 1930s. *Photo reproduced by permission of the Corbis Corporation.*

Francis Everett Townsend (1867–1960) Francis Everett Townsend became a champion of the elderly when he was himself an old man. Angry at the way old people were ignored and abandoned, he lobbied in 1933 that all retirees should receive sixty dollars a week from the time they turned sixty years old. Partly because of Townsend's public outcry, New Dealers in government made a small pension, an amount much smaller than Townsend proposed, a part of the Social Security Act of 1935. *Photo courtesy of the Library of Congress.*

❖ SLEEPING THROUGH SURGERY

The use of anesthetics is one of America's most important contributions to medicine. In 1844, in Hartford, Connecticut, dentist Horace Wells (1815–1848) used nitrous oxide (laughing gas) to sedate patients while extracting teeth. In Boston, in 1846, another dentist, William T. G. Morton (1819–1868), used ether during an operation at Massachusetts General Hospital. In the 1930s, both of these anesthetics were widely used. But gradually, amazing stories about a new generation of anesthetics began to appear in the press. In 1933, a patient in New York read a newspaper during an operation. Surgeons made headlines performing operations on themselves. And during brain surgery, patients were reported to be chatting with nurses and doctors.

At the start of the 1930s, the most effective anesthetic was ether. Chloroform was popular in Europe, but it was dangerous. If the dose was even slightly too high, it could stop the patient's heart. Ether carried risks too. It caused stomach problems and could make patients excitable and difficult to control. Patients who needed several operations became tolerant of ether, so it stopped working at low doses. Worst of all, ether was unstable. Sparks from X-ray machines and other equipment could cause an explosion. Anesthetists became skilled at controlling ether. Patients would be put to sleep using nitrous oxide, then kept under using ether. Nitrous oxide would be used in the closing stages of the operation to stop vomiting. Anesthetists had to watch the patient carefully for signs of problems and reduce or increase the dose of anesthetic depending on the type and sensitivity of the tissue being cut through by the surgeon.

Ether, chloroform, and nitrous oxide were effective, but crude. Causing someone to lose consciousness is in any case highly dangerous, and many patients reacted badly to these basic drugs. In the early 1930s, a French drug called neocaine appeared. When injected into the spine, neocaine allowed surgeons to work on the legs and lower body while the patient was awake. Another new drug, Avertin, arrived from Germany in 1930 and could be used for short operations. Pernocton knocked out the patient safely for several hours and made more complex surgery possible. Pernocton was so safe it was used for surgery on pregnant women and during childbirth. Novocaine, eucaine, and benzyl alcohol were all "local" anesthetics. Novocaine was the drug used by the surgeons who operated on themselves. But most impressive of all was diothane, which appeared in 1938. Developed in Cincinnati, Ohio, diothane was longer lasting than novocaine and was nonaddictive.

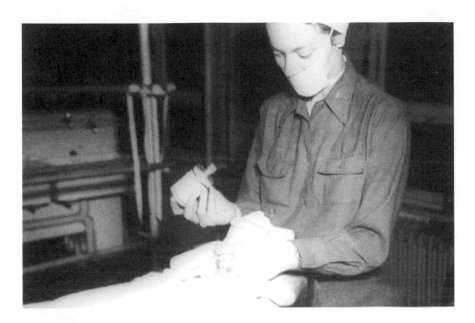

By 1930, ether was widely used by doctors and nurses to anesthetize (put to sleep) surgical patients. Reproduced by permission of Visual Image Presentations.

While surgeons became more skillful, anesthetics made surgery more comfortable. Before the 1930s, nurses made sure the correct amount of anesthetic was delivered. While nurse anesthetists continued to work in the 1930s, the job of the anesthetist became more skilled and more complex. As local anesthetics became available, the practice of anesthetics became one of the medical specialties. While surgery became more impressive during the 1930s and surgeons were turned into heroes, it was often forgotten that without anesthetics and skilled anesthetists many operations would have been impossible.

❖ BIRTH CONTROL: PUBLIC NUISANCE OR PUBLIC HEALTH ISSUE?

Working as a nurse in the slums of New York City, Margaret Sanger (1879–1966) realized that proper birth control could save many lives. Deaths during pregnancy and childbirth were common. But more shocking was the fact that a quarter of such deaths happened when women tried to end their pregnancies. Many performed abortions on themselves or went to illegal clinics where hygiene standards were poor. In 1916, Sanger opened a birth control clinic in Brooklyn, New York, with the aim of telling women how to avoid pregnancy in the first place. She was arrested for causing a public nuisance. By 1938, largely as a result of Sanger's campaigning, the right to receive information about birth control methods was part of federal law. Only three states, Connecticut, Mississippi, and Massachusetts, did not allow medical workers to offer such advice.

Until the 1930s, birth control information and contraceptive devices were illegal. The U.S. Penal Code decreed that anyone caught in possession of contraceptive articles could be fined up to $5,000 and jailed for five years. Even married couples were forbidden from buying condoms. Even so, many doctors broke the law and prescribed contraceptives. In 1930, when it was clear that the law had become unenforceable, the National Committee on Federal Legislation for Birth Control recommended that federal restrictions be ended. Their twenty million members filed 325,000 endorsements with Congress. On November 30, 1936 the federal courts of appeal agreed that birth control did not fall under the obscenity laws. In June 1937 the American Medical Association (AMA) approved birth control, advising physicians of their legal rights when they prescribed contraceptives.

In 1938 birth control advice and contraceptives were still forbidden in Connecticut, Mississippi, and Massachusetts. Seven birth control clinics operated in Connecticut and were tolerated by the state authorities, although the use of contraceptives remained illegal. In Mississippi, even spoken advice was banned. Three clinics were raided in 1937, and their staff arrested and fined. The remaining five Massachusetts clinics were closed down. Margaret Sanger (1879–1966) continued to campaign. By the end of the decade, she had succeeded in making birth control an important part of modern medicine. In doing so, she saved many lives.

❖ PAYING FOR HEALTH CARE

Before the Depression, hospitals were funded from several sources. Most of their income came from endowments, which are investments given to them by wealthy supporters. They also depended on charitable gifts and the fees paid by patients. After the stock market crash of 1929, endowment income fell. The Depression also reduced the amount of money coming from charities. Between October 1929 and October 1930, the amount paid to hospitals for each patient fell from $236.12 to $59.26. But most worrisome of all was the drop in income from fees. It was a sign that people were going without proper medical care because they couldn't afford to pay for it. As a way of solving this problem, voluntary hospitals, where patients had to pay fees, turned to insurance schemes to preserve their income. Labor unions and other organizations also offered prepayment schemes. But in the middle of the Depression, few people signed up.

The Blue Cross insurance program was developed by the American Hospital Association (AHA) in 1933. For a monthly fee subscribers could have three weeks of hospital care paid for by Blue Cross. One of the principles of the scheme was that it would not make a profit. All the money

The Cost of Being Sick

In 1938, the minimum wage was set at forty cents per hour. This meant that a worker making the minimum wage earned around $800 per year. At the same time, medical costs were high. The cost of treatment for common medical conditions was as follows:

Measles:	$4.81
Chicken Pox:	$1.82
Whooping Cough:	$6.27
Broken Limb:	$18.07
Childbirth:	$98.74
Heart Disease:	$49.56
Pneumonia:	$58.72

The average American could count on being unable to work through illness for eight days in each year. Treatment for a minor respiratory disease cost $5.91, and for a stomach upset, $6.89. The cost of staying in hospital, excluding any medical fees, cost around four dollars a day in a nine-bed ward.

Source: *Statistical Abstract of the United States, 1940.* Washington, DC: U.S. Government Printing Office, 1941.

went into paying hospital charges. What Blue Cross did not pay for was physicians' bills. In 1939 Blue Shield was set up to cover the cost of surgery and other treatments. Blue Shield began in California, at the same time as another prepayment plan began in Michigan. The idea soon spread around the country.

By the late 1930s, doctors and other health workers endorsed voluntary health insurance such as the "Blues." The main advantage for health professionals was that it allowed them to continue in well-paid private practice. Insurance companies offered their own schemes, usually at greater cost, but Blue Cross and Blue Shield allowed the fee-for-service health system to survive the Depression. In Europe, countries were moving toward national health insurance schemes run by central governments and paid for through taxation. The success of the "Blues" in the 1930s is the main reason why the United States kept its voluntary hospitals and independent physicians.

Founded in 1846, by 1930 the American Medical Association (AMA) was a powerful political force. It controlled medical schools and dominated private medical practice. The AMA saw insurance schemes as a threat to doctors' freedom. It even argued that if the government or insurance companies paid medical bills, doctors would become bored and unimaginative. Because it supported insurance schemes, the Roosevelt administration was accused of trying to turn doctors into "mere laborers." The Depression made it necessary for state and federal government to be involved in funding medical services. The Farm Security Administration, for example, made deals with local medical associations to keep fees low for farm workers. When this happened, the AMA stepped in to keep fees up. In 1934, the AMA advised medical schools to limit the number of medical students. The effect of this was to reduce the number of doctors and keep fees high.

In the late 1930s, pressure grew for a national health bill. The AMA was strongly opposed to anything it saw as a challenge to physicians' freedom. Fearing that a compulsory insurance scheme would be put in place, the AMA decided to relax its stand on voluntary insurance. Partly through the efforts of the AMA, Senator Robert Wagner's 1939 health insurance bill, which proposed a compulsory national health insurance system administered by the states, was quietly dropped.

❖ SULFA DRUGS

Before the 1930s there was no treatment for infectious diseases such as bacterial meningitis. Many people were killed by diseases that are easily treated in the twenty-first century. In 1932, the German chemist Gerhard Domagk (1895–1964) discovered that a dye called Prontosil killed the streptococcus bacteria. The active ingredient in the dye was sulfanilamide. Prontosil arrived in the United States in 1936. Perrin H. Long (1899–1965) began using it at Johns Hopkins University Hospital.

The sulfonamides, or "sulfa" drugs, seemed to be a miracle cure for a whole range of diseases. But there were problems. Some patients suffered kidney failure when treated with sulfa drugs, while others developed skin lesions and high fever. Certain diseases, such as gonorrhea, began to resist sulfa treatments, while others could not be treated at all. Then, in 1937, a chemist working in Bristol, Tennessee, made a terrible mistake. He discovered that sulfanilamide could be dissolved by a chemical called diethylene glycol. The advantage of this was that it could then be given to patients in liquid form. The "elixir" was tested for fragrance and taste and found acceptable. Unfortunately, diethylene glycol is a poison. By the

D r. Alphonse Raymond Dochez (1882–1964) was professor of medicine at Columbia University. He spent many years working on a vaccine against the common cold virus. The problem was that there was no filter fine enough to trap it. Even if there had been, no microscope was powerful enough to see it. In 1935, Dochez managed to catch some of the cold virus. For the first time, he managed to grow the virus outside the body, on a diet of chicken embryos. But making the vaccine was another matter. More than sixty years later, at the beginning of the twenty-first century, there was still no vaccine, and no cure, for the common cold.

time the Federal Drug Administration (FDA) found out, approximately 107 people had been killed by the medicine, including many children.

Before 1938, drug manufacturers did not have to disclose what was in their products unless the products contained narcotics. As long as their claims were not fraudulent, drug companies were free to say anything they liked about the powers of their medicines. The sulfa "elixir" scandal inspired Congress to amend the 1906 Pure Food and Drug Act. On June 27, 1938, President Roosevelt (1882–1945) signed the Food, Drug, and Cosmetic Act, one of the last New Deal measures. The Act banned misleading advertising and stated that labels had to carry clear warnings about the risks involved in taking certain drugs. All ingredients had to be listed. Most importantly, no new drug could go on the market until the FDA was happy that it was safe. The new law also applied to processed food and cosmetics. In fact, the first seizure made by the FDA under the new law was an "eyelash beautifier" that could cause blindness.

❖ THE TROUBLE WITH TUBERCULOSIS AND POLIO

In 1936, the U.S. Bureau of the Census estimated that of every twenty-one deaths in the United States, one was from tuberculosis (TB). Also known as consumption, phthisis, and the "great white plague," TB most commonly affects the lungs. It is transmitted when sufferers cough up the germs, which are then breathed in by others. In the 1930s, cures for TB did not exist. Patients were sent away to TB hospitals, or sanitoriums, where they had plenty of rest, fresh air, and a good diet. Sometimes the diseased parts of the lungs were removed in surgery. But most patients either recovered on their own or died.

With no cure available, the effort to stamp out TB focused on prevention. The earlier the disease was discovered, the more likely it was that the patient would survive. It also meant that people who had the disease could be kept away from those who didn't. X-ray machines already enabled doctors to see when lungs had been infected. During the 1930s, X-ray technology improved dramatically, and this helped doctors slow down the spread tuberculosis. In 1933, an X-ray machine that could take four pictures a minute made it possible for large numbers of people to be screened. School children lined up to be "shot" with portable X-ray machines. It was also discovered that TB could be transmitted through cow's milk. Tubercular cows were destroyed and milk was pasteurized to kill off any bacteria. In 1930, seventy out of every one hundred thousand Americans died from TB. By 1938, the death rate had fallen to fifty-six in every one hundred thousand.

Poliomyelitis, also known as infantile paralysis and polio, is a vicious disease. It can be fatal, but more often it cripples its victims for life. Usually polio has been a disease of the young, but its most famous victim was President Franklin D. Roosevelt (1882–1945). He was struck by the disease at the age of thirty-nine and left a paraplegic. Somehow he managed to conceal the extent of his disability. He wore strong leg braces and walked by swinging his hips while balancing with a cane. During his political career he was photographed in a wheelchair only once. Even so, Roosevelt worked hard for a cure. He spent most of his personal fortune on the rehabilitation organization Warm Springs Foundation and gave his name to a national fundraising campaign that held events on his birthday, January 30.

In 1938, Roosevelt's support for the Warm Springs Foundation helped it expand to the national level. It became the National Foundation for Infantile Paralysis. A lawyer, Basil O'Connor (1892–1972), took charge. His fundraising campaign became known as the "March of Dimes," because it collected small change from millions of donors. At basketball games a canvas would be laid on the court during half time to catch coins thrown by spectators. A Disney cartoon featuring Mickey Mouse, Donald Duck, and others, included the song:

> Heigh-ho, heigh-ho
> We'll lick old polio,
> With dimes and quarters
> And our doll-aaars…
> Ho, heigh-ho!

The March of Dimes was the most successful health fundraising campaign of the 1930s. It funded research into cures for polio and the ways it was spread. This research would eventually lead to the successful polio vaccine in the 1950s.

❖ SEXUALLY TRANSMITTED DISEASES

By the 1930s, many infectious diseases, such as typhoid, dysentery, and diphtheria, did not pose a major threat to public health. But venereal diseases (VD), transmitted through sexual contact, were out of control. There were no effective drug treatments for the major venereal diseases. Even if there had been, many Americans were too embarrassed or ashamed to seek help. Public health campaigns begun during World War I had all but failed by 1930. In 1935, the sexually transmitted disease syphilis brought disability or death to more than half a million Americans.

The spread of diseases such as syphilis and gonorrhea was made worse by the breakdown of family life during the Depression. Support for research into cures was hampered by the idea that victims of VD got what they deserved. Yet millions of dollars were spent on treatments costing up to one thousand dollars per patient. Recognizing this as a waste of money and human life, Surgeon General Thomas Parran (1892–1968) believed that VD could be controlled by changing people's behavior. By 1938, couples had to have "clean" medical certificates before they were allowed to marry. Postgraduate courses on venereal disease were set up at medical schools to educate doctors. Parran argued for federal funds to fight VD, but public opinion held back reform. In the 1930s, most Americans were ignorant, afraid, and ashamed of VD. It remained out of control for several decades more.

❖ PSYCHOANALYSIS

Psychoanalysis is a system of solving psychological problems by identifying and confronting moments of conflict in the patient's past. It began in Europe at the beginning of the twentieth century and began to catch on in the United States in the 1930s. In 1933, the Nazis labeled psychoanalysis the "Jewish science" and burned literature pertaining to it. Many Jewish psychoanalysts fled to the United States and began to practice there. Immigrant analysts, such as René Spitz, Else Frenkel-Brunswick, Ernst Kris, and Kä the Wolf, helped to revolutionize the study and treatment of personality disorders in the United States. They made the United States the world center for psychoanalysis and psychotherapy.

❖ THE MEDICAL PROFESSION IN THE 1930s

As medical research uncovered new ways of dealing with sickness and disease, medicine became increasingly complex. By 1930, physicians had to

*Public health posters
warned Americans
about outbreaks of
diseases. Courtesy of the
Library of Congress.*

How to Avoid a Malpractice Lawsuit

By 1935, doctors were increasingly being sued for malpractice. A doctor writing in *Clinical Medicine and Surgery* gave the following advice on how to avoid being sued:

Never promise a cure.

Always select specialists who know more than you do.

If things have gone wrong, do not tell anyone until you know what the end result will be.

End your relationship with any patient who seems likely to go to the law.

Make sure that any sponges used in an operation are counted before the wound is stitched up."

Source: "Malpractice Protection." *Time* (November 18, 1935): p. 54.

understand a huge range of techniques, treatments, drugs, and ailments. Specialist clinics and hospitals sprang up, and the cost of treatment rose sharply. The difficulty of making sure patients had the best possible care was made worse by the pay-per-treatment system. This system meant that doctors and patients had to choose between the best treatment and what the patient could afford. Another major challenge facing the American medical profession in the 1930s was how to organize itself more efficiently. Health professionals opposed outside regulation, especially by federal government. They managed to avoid it by becoming more specialized and more professional.

General practitioners (GPs) had difficulty collecting their bills during the Depression. Among physicians, they earned the least, while surgeons and specialists earned the most. In 1930, specialist doctors in Wisconsin earned as much as $20,000 per year, around five times the average for doctors overall. As a result of this, tension developed between GPs and specialists. In Britain, patients had to be referred to a specialist by a GP. But in the United States, there was nothing to stop specialists from taking patients on themselves. Many GPs saw this as an opportunity to make money and began calling themselves specialists. It was only in the 1930s that the American Medical Association required specialists to be tested on their skills and abilities.

Under the control of the American Medical Association (AMA), so-called "specialty boards" began to regulate the medical profession. The

1930s saw the birth of the American Board of Obstetrics and Gynecology, Internal Medicine, Surgery, Pediatrics, and many others. Each of these boards made sure that the quality of its members was maintained. Members of the board had to go through three years of training in their specialty after their general medical training or internship. Yet many problems remained. The boards themselves controlled their own standards and were not regulated from outside. Physicians had managed to stay beyond the prying eyes of federal government and the American public. Despite many improvements, the medical profession was still unregulated and disorganized by the end of the decade.

 For More Information

BOOKS

Allen, Frederick Lewis. *Since Yesterday: The 1930s in America, September 3, 1929–September 3, 1939.* New York: HarperCollins, 1986.

Bender, Lionel. *Frontiers of Medicine.* New York: Gloucester Press, 1991.

Bryan, Jenny. *The History of Health and Medicine.* Austin, TX: Raintree Steck-Vaughn, 1996.

Burge, Michael C. and Don Nardo. *Vaccines: Preventing Disease.* San Diego, CA: Lucent Books, 1992.

Cohen, Daniel. *The Last 100 Years: Medicine.* New York: M. Evans, 1981.

Cook, Chris, and David Waller, editors. *The Longman Handbook of Modern American History, 1763–1996.* New York: Longman, 1998.

Cowley, Malcolm. *Think Back on Us—A Contemporary Chronicle of the 1930s.* Carbondale, IL: Southern Illinois University Press, 1967.

Cunningham, Robert, III, and Robert Cunningham Jr. *The Blues: A History of the Blue Cross and Blue Shield System.* DeKalb, IL: Northern Illinois University Press, 1997.

Dowswell, Paul. *Medicine.* Chicago: Heinemann Library, 2001.

Feinstein, Stephen. *The 1930s: From the Great Depression to the Wizard of Oz (Decades of the Twentieth Century).* New York: Enslow Publishers, 2001.

Garza, Hedda. *Women in Medicine.* New York: Franklin Watts, 1994.

Gottfried, Ted. *Alexander Fleming: Discoverer of Penicillin.* New York: Franklin Watts, 1997.

Jones, Constance. *Karen Horney.* New York: Chelsea House, 1989.

Landau, Elaine. *Tuberculosis.* New York: F. Watts, 1995.

Miller, Brandon Marie. *Just What the Doctor Ordered: The History of American Medicine.* Minneapolis, MN: Lerner Publications, 1997.

Parker, Steve. *Medical Advances*. Austin, TX: Raintree Steck-Vaughn, 1998.

Royston, Angela. *100 Greatest Medical Discoveries*. Danbury, CT: Grolier Educational, 1997.

Sayers, Janet. *Mothers of Psychoanalysis: Helen Deutsch, Karen Horney, Anna Freud, and Melanie Klein*. New York: W. W. Norton, 1993.

Scheehan, Angela, editor. *The Marshall Cavendish Encyclopedia of Health*. New York: M. Cavendish, 1995.

Sherrow, Victoria. *Hardship and Hope: America and the Great Depression*. New York: Twenty-First Century Books, 1997.

Silverstein, Alvin, et al. *Polio*. Berkeley Heights, NJ: Enslow Publishers, 2001.

Stille, Darlene R. *Extraordinary Women of Medicine*. New York: Children's Press, 1997.

Whitelaw, Nancy. *Margaret Sanger: Every Child a Wanted Child*. New York: Dillon Press, 1994.

Yount, Lisa. *Disease Detectives*. San Diego: Lucent Books, 2000.

Yount, Lisa. *History of Medicine*. San Diego: Lucent Books, 2001.

PERIODICALS

Stone, Hannah M. "Birth Control Wins." *The Nation* (January 16, 1937, Vol. 144, No. 3): pp. 70–71.

WEB SITES

American Red Cross History: 1920–1939. http://www.redcross.org/museum/19201939b.html (accessed July 23, 2002).

Blue Cross and Blue Shield History. http://www.bcbs.com/whoweare/history.html (accessed July 23, 2002).

March of Dimes History and Mission. http://www.modimes.org/AboutUs/4220.htm (accessed July 23, 2002).

National Institute of Standards and Technology: The Depression. http://www.100.nist.gov/depression.htm (accessed July 23, 2002).

New Deal Network. http://newdeal.feri.org/ (accessed July 23, 2002).

The Pharmaceutical Century: 1920s and 1930s. http://pubs.acs.org/journals/pharmcent/Ch2.html (accessed July 23, 2002).

Science and Technology

1930: The gas Freon is manufactured in large quantities for use in refrigerators and air conditioners.

1930: Sliced bread becomes available in American supermarkets.

1930: Transcontinental and West Airlines offers the first New York to Los Angeles air service.

1930: February 18 Clyde William Tombaugh confirms the existence of Pluto, the ninth planet in the solar system.

1930: April 4 The American Interplanetary Society (later the American Rocket Society) is set up to promote the idea of interplanetary exploration.

1931: January 2 Ernest O. Lawrence invents the cyclotron, a machine that makes possible high-energy physics, including, in the next decade, the atomic bomb.

1931: May 27 At the Langley Memorial Aeronautical Laboratory in Hampton, Virginia, engineers begin to test airplanes in a wind tunnel.

1931: December 28 The George Westinghouse Bridge on the Philadelphia-Pittsburgh turnpike is built using the largest concrete arch in the United States.

1932: Ford introduces its V8 engine to replace the underpowered four-cylinder engine of the Model A.

1932: RCA introduces the first cathode-ray television.

1932: August 25 Amelia Earhart makes the first nonstop transcontinental flight from Los Angeles to Newark. It takes her nineteen hours and five minutes.

1932: December 1 The U.S. Department of Commerce begins the first weather map service using a teletypewriter to print maps at remote locations.

1933: The speed of light is calculated at 186,000 miles per second.

1933: To market its newly invented smokeless gunpowder, the DuPont Company buys the Remington Arms Company.

1933: Albert Einstein immigrates to the United States. He takes up a professorship at Princeton University's Institute for Advanced Studies.

1934: April 4 The American-built airship *Akron* crashes at sea, killing seventy-three crew members.

1934: Chrysler and DeSoto introduce streamlined "Airflow" automobiles with automatic transmission.

1934: The Federal Communications Commission is set up to oversee the national phone service.

1934: A tethered bathysphere, a steel sphere lowered from a ship, descends to a depth of 1,001 meters. Making up its two-man crew are Charles William Beebe and Otis Barton.

1934: **November 29** In New York, the American Polar Society is founded.

1935: The first canned beer goes on sale in the United States.

1935: **November 11** The balloon *Explorer II* and its two-man crew reach a record altitude of 13.71 miles, or 72,395 feet. The flight is sponsored by the National Geographic Society and the U.S. Army Air Corps.

1936: **March 1** The Boulder Canyon Dam (later the Hoover Dam) is completed. The reservoir it creates, called Lake Mead, is the largest reservoir in the world.

1936: **November 23** The U.S. Patent Office celebrates its centenary with the introduction of the fluorescent light bulb.

1937: Ford customers have the choice of sixty or eighty-five horsepower motors. Buick and Oldsmobile offer automatic transmission, while the steering column gearshift is reintroduced.

1937: IBM devises a "collating machine" that records information on punch cards. It is used by the federal government to keep the employment records of twenty-six million Americans. Without machines such as this many government programs of the late 1930s would be impossible.

1937: **May 6** The German airship *Hindenberg* catches fire upon landing at Lakehurst, New Jersey.

1938: Nylon-bristled toothbrushes become the first consumer product made with DuPont's newly patented nylon.

1938: **October 22** The first "xerox" copy is made by Chester F. Carlson. His copying machine uses a process called xerography.

1939: The first jet engine is fitted to a German Heinkel 179 aircraft and makes a successful flight in August.

1939: Life in American kitchens is never the same again after the introduction of the electric knife.

1939: **April 4** Western Union introduces a system that allows six-by-seven-inch photographs to be sent by cable. The first picture is sent from London to New York and is published in American newspapers.

1939: **August 2** Albert Einstein writes President Franklin D. Roosevelt to advise funding research on the atomic bomb.

1939: **September 14** The first mass-produced helicopter, designed by Igor Sikorsky, begins test flights.

1939: **October 31** At the end of its first year, the New York World's Fair has had almost twenty-six million visitors.

✳ *Overview* . . . .

Despite, or maybe because of, the Depression, Americans showed great interest in the future in the 1930s. World's Fairs, such as the Century of Progress exposition in Chicago (1933–34), were packed with exhibits predicting technological advances. Science and technology were also seen as the path to a better society. Skyscrapers, airplanes, automobiles, and advances in physics and biology all seemed good reasons to be optimistic about the future.

Even after the stock market crash of 1929, scientific and technological research carried on. The sponsorship by institutions, such as the Rockefeller Institute, which were unaffected by market conditions, made possible so many technological advances that the 1930s became known as "the machine age." Major advances were made in atomic physics, as well as in plastics and synthetic materials. Out of this activity came a new group calling themselves "technocrats." Technocrats believed that new scientific advances would provide the tools to end the Depression and solve the problems of society. Technocrats could be found everywhere, from church pulpits to universities and the press. The idea of machines taking over for humans in routine jobs was highly attractive. Low-cost, mass-produced household goods seemed to offer a better life for everyone. In the early 1930s, the use of plastics such as a product called Bakelite offered a new world of cheap, stylish, mass-produced goods.

The machine age influenced housing in several ways. Most importantly, it inspired the idea that, like machines, communities could be designed.

The Bauhaus movement designed buildings constructed as efficiently as possible, with residents sharing communal spaces. Swiss architect Le Corbusier even talked about buildings as "machines for living." But the most obvious influence of the machine age on housing was prefabrication. "Ready-to-build" units arrived on trucks and were constructed in a matter of hours. As one slogan put it, houses could be "built like Fords." In the end, none of these solutions worked very well. During the Depression, people with the money to buy a house wanted something more substantial than a prefab, while large-scale housing projects often ignored the needs of the people who had to live in them.

The machine age had its critics. British author Aldous Huxley published *Brave New World* in 1932. In the novel, humans have become slaves to machines. Other authors, such as the poet John Drinkwater, took a similar view of machines. Better known is Charlie Chaplin's 1936 film, *Modern Times*. Chaplin used his film to attack big business and mass-production. He plays a production line worker who ends up being sucked into the giant machine and is trapped among the cogs and gears. Despite moments of hilarious comedy, the serious message of the film is obvious. The power of the film's message is increased because it was the first film in which Chaplin uses sound technology to speak. Chaplin's movie highlighted the contrast between the benefits of scientific and technological advances and the problems caused when they were put to use. The machine age of the 1930s offered Americans huge technological gains, but it also forced Americans to think about the responsibilities that went along with "progress." In the next decade, the atomic bomb would soon illustrate the weight of those responsibilities.

Ruth Benedict (1887–1948) Anthropologist Ruth Benedict attended Vassar College and graduated in 1909, entering Columbia's Ph.D. program in 1921. Through her work she campaigned for women's rights and against racism. She was an early advocate of the idea that what is unacceptable in one culture might be acceptable in another. Such views made her a controversial figure in the 1930s. But her work on the differences between cultures was a major influence on anthropology, political thought, and cultural studies in the decades that followed. *Photo reproduced by permission of the Corbis Corporation.*

Richard E. Byrd (1888–1957) After retiring through injury from active service in the U.S. Navy, Richard E. Byrd pursued his interest in exploration. In 1926 he flew to the North Pole, but in the 1930s switched his attention to the Antarctic. Admiral Byrd flew many times to the South Pole, bringing equipment to teams stationed there and providing better living conditions. His flights also began the process of surveying Antarctica. One of the ironies of Byrd's achievements is that by bringing technology to the continent, they helped bring an end to the era of the great explorers. *Photo courtesy of the Library of Congress.*

Amelia Earhart (1897–1937) Amelia Earhart grew up in a well-off Kansas family and first took to the air in 1920 on a pleasure trip. In October 1922, she set her first record, reaching 14,000 feet without wearing an oxygen mask. By the late 1920s the public knew her as "Lady Lindy," a name that stuck when she matched Charles Lindbergh's solo crossing of the Atlantic in 1932. After setting a series of records she disappeared in 1937 while crossing the Pacific. Earhart saw aviation as an arena where men and women could be equal. She succeeded in becoming one of its greatest pioneers. *Photo reproduced by permission of the Granger Collection, Ltd.*

Philo T. Farnsworth (1906–1971) Often overlooked in the history of television, Philo T. Farnsworth is one of its most important developers. A student at Brigham Young University at the age of sixteen, he soon after designed a system for transmitting moving pictures over the airwaves. He transmitted his first television picture in 1927. Farnsworth was dogged by legal battles with RCA, his major competitor. They finally settled on a joint patent for television, and Farnsworth shared RCA's profits on the system. He was one of the last great independent inventors, holding more than 135 patents in television and other areas. *Photo courtesy of the Library of Congress.*

Theodore von Kármán (1881–1963) Born in Budapest, Hungary, Theodore von Kármán immigrated to California in 1929, where he worked as an aeronautical engineer. He was a key figure in making California the center of the American aviation industry. The Kármán law of turbulence influenced the distinctive shape of the Douglas DC-3 airliner. A teacher at the California Institute of Technology, Kármán managed to have a major influence in all areas of aeronautics. His interest in rocketry earned him membership of what was known at Caltech as the "Suicide Club." But the risks he took with experimental rockets laid the foundation for the space programs of the 1960s. *Photo courtesy of the Library of Congress.*

Robert A. Millikan (1868–1953) In 1923 Robert A. Millikan received the Nobel Prize in physics for his work on Albert Einstein's quantum theory. But his influence on American science was also as an administrator. Under his guidance, Throop College of Technology in Pasadena was renamed the California Institute of Technology. By the 1930s, the name "Caltech" had become a byword for American scientific research. Millikan continued teaching and researching, building Caltech into a world-class institution. He also worked hard to convince the American public of the importance of science. *Photo courtesy of the Library of Congress.*

Harold C. Urey (1893–1981) Harold C. Urey majored in biology at the University of Montana. He earned his Ph.D. from the University of California, Berkeley, in 1921, after just two years of study. He received the Nobel Prize in chemistry in 1934 for the discovery of Deuterium, or "heavy water," used in developing the atomic bomb. After the bombing of Hiroshima and Nagasaki, Urey campaigned for the control of nuclear power. He was known as a generous man, devoting a great deal of time to his graduate students and loaning money to other scientists to help with their research. *Photo courtesy of the Library of Congress.*

John von Neumann (1903–1957) Born in Hungary, John von Neumann received his Ph.D. in mathematics from Budapest University at the age of twenty-three. He made contributions in a huge number of fields, including chemical engineering, quantum physics, mathematics, economics, logic, and computing. His work on game theory, which describes decision-making processes, remains influential in the twenty-first century. In the 1940s he worked on the atomic bomb and became a member of the Atomic Energy Commission in 1954. *Photo reproduced by permission of the Corbis Corporation.*

◆◆ *Topics in the News* . . . .

❖ FLYING HIGH

During the 1930s two airborne technologies rivalled each other. Airplanes became sleeker, faster, and more comfortable as the decade progressed. But airships, also known as "dirigibles" and today known as "blimps," could cover huge distances, staying aloft for sixty or more hours at a time. Both forms of air travel received widespread publicity, though the airplane finally won the hearts of the American public.

"Fixed-wing" aviation—airplanes—received a boost in 1932 when Governor of New York Franklin D. Roosevelt (1882–1945) flew to Chicago to accept the Democratic presidential nomination. Roosevelt's trip illustrated that air travel could be a useful form of everyday transport. But it was aviators such as Wiley Post (1899–1935) who pushed airplane technology to its limits and won the hearts of Americans. Post flew around the globe in nine days in 1931 and in eight days the following year. In 1938, Howard Hughes (1905–1976) cut the record to four days. A successful businessman, Hughes's experience would make him a major influence on American commercial airlines in years to come. Flying also gave women the chance to hit the headlines. In 1932, Amelia Earhart (1897–1937) became the first woman to fly solo across the Atlantic. In the following years she set many distance and speed records but disappeared over the Pacific Ocean in 1937 while trying to become the first woman to fly around the world.

Perhaps the greatest American hero of the decade was Charles Lindbergh (1902–1974). In 1927 Lindbergh became the first person to fly solo across the Atlantic. During the Depression, Lindbergh's heroic exploits were front-page news. He and his plane, the *Spirit of St. Louis,* became a modern symbol of the pioneering spirit. With his wife, Anne Morrow Lindbergh (1906–2001), he flew many long-distance flights, gathering experience that would make him American Airways' most valuable adviser.

The National Advisory Committee on Aeronautics (NACA) spent the 1930s advising airplane manufacturers on streamlining and engine development. The airlines wanted bigger, faster, more comfortable machines, such as the ten-passenger Boeing 247. The Douglas Company built its DC-1 to compete with Boeing's most up-to-date planes. Like the 247, it boasted an all-metal skin and powerful engines. It could carry twelve passengers and first flew in July 1933. But even as the DC-1 was being tested, the decision had been made to turn it into the DC-2, the fastest passenger airliner of its day. A larger version of the DC-2, known as the DC-3, offered fourteen sleeper berths and could seat twenty-one passengers in its "day version." The DC-3, known as the "Gooney Bird" because of its curving wings, sold to airlines around the world. It was tough, fast, and reliable. Many DC-3s remain in service in the twenty-first century, making it one of the most successful aircraft ever built.

While fixed-wing airliners were becoming the flying machine of choice, airship technology had also made advances. Rigid airships or "dirigibles" were crafted as huge cigar-shaped structures filled with hydrogen gas that gave lift to a gondola that carried passengers and crew. The main advantage of airships over fixed-wing airplanes is that they can spend days in flight without refueling.

Most airship development in the 1930s went on in Germany. But after the *Los Angeles* was bought from the Germans by the U.S. Navy, two American airships were planned. The *Akron* and the *Macon* cost $8 million each and were built at Akron, Ohio, between March 1930 and August 1931. The *Akron* was intended as an aircraft carrier. A system of hooks allowed small fixed-wing aircraft to be launched and recovered while in flight. Both the *Akron* and *Macon* were destroyed in crashes. The *Akron* went down in 1933 with the loss of seventy-three lives, while the *Macon* crashed in the Pacific near San Diego, killing two crew members.

Before long-range airliners began operating in the 1950s, flying boats carried passengers along the trans-ocean routes. The Sikorsky S-42, the Martin Clippers, and the Boeing 314 offered great comfort and style. They were the second most luxurious way to fly in the 1930s. Their advantage was that they needed no special airstrip to take off and land, just a strip of open water, such as a lake.

By far the most luxurious way to fly in the 1930s was by airship. The German airship *Hindenberg* began a transatlantic service in 1936 and made

Howard Hughes, an influential millionaire, owned several large planes and boats, including the flying boat called the Spruce Goose. Reproduced by permission of AP/Wide World Photo.

Railroad companies responded to their difficulties by modernizing. Lines were electrified, and companies such as the Baltimore and Ohio brought in the "refrigerated principle," air conditioning whole trains by the late 1930s. On the Minneapolis to Chicago line the Zephyr Streamliner set new standards in speed and reliability. It was on time even in the depths of winter and could average eighty miles an hour. Over long distances rail could compete with trucking. The railroad companies improved the pickup and delivery systems at their freight yards. Improving the relationship between rail and road transportation became an important goal of President Franklin D. Roosevelt's New Deal. Roosevelt (1882–1945) signed the Railroad Reorganization Bill on June 16, 1933.

In 1930 there were 325,000 miles of state and federal roads. But only two-thirds of that distance was surfaced. This placed severe restrictions on road transport, especially for long-distance trucks. The National Industrial Recovery Act (NIRA) allowed the federal government to organize the unemployed into work parties to repair and resurface the roads. New parkways and turnpikes were built to carry the increasing volume of road traffic. More than half a million unemployed men were put to work building roads in the 1930s.

❖ CHEMISTRY INFLUENCES AMERICAN SCIENCE

By the end of the 1930s, chemistry was a major discipline in American science. In 1930, American universities awarded 332 Ph.D.s in chemistry. In 1939, that number was 532. American chemists won several important awards in the 1930s, and the number of industrial laboratories grew. Between 1928 and 1938, Dow Chemical increased the number of its research workers from 100 to 500.

An increase in researchers led to an increase in new discoveries. For example, discoveries were made during the 1930s about the chemical elements that make up the basic building blocks of the universe. The "periodic table," devised in 1869, lists these elements according to their "atomic number." By 2001, there were 103 known elements, but in the 1930s only 92 were known, and numbers 61, 85, and 87 were missing. Marguerite Perey (1909–1975) discovered number 87 in 1939, naming it Francium after her native France. In 1935, Jeffrey Dempster (1886–1950) discovered that the element uranium occasionally appeared in a different form or "isotope" called uranium-235. This is the substance used in the atomic bomb.

Perhaps one of the most important advances in chemistry during the 1930s was the commercial production of vitamins. The existence of vitamins had been verified in the 1900s. But nothing was known about their

Refrigerators had been around since the 1920s, but they only became widespread after 1930. One reason was that most homes outside of major cities did not have electricity. But early refrigerators were rather dangerous. In 1930 Thomas Midgley (1899–1944) managed to create Freon, an odorless gas that was thought to be safe. More than a million refrigerators were sold in 1930, over three quarters for household kitchens. Americans spent more than $220 million on refrigerators that year. By 1931, 14.7 percent of American homes had a refrigerator. Most of them were in urban areas.

chemical makeup until the 1930s. Paul Karrer (1889–1971) "discovered" the structure of vitamin C in his laboratory at Birmingham University in England, and Norman Haworth (1883–1950) of Zurich University in Switzerland studied the make up of vitamin A and B2. For their efforts both chemists won a Nobel Prize in 1937.

Chemical research also became crucial to American industry during the 1930s. The chemical company DuPont introduced "duprene," a synthetic rubber, in 1931. The new material had several advantages over natural rubber. Duprene did not degrade when exposed to air, kerosene, or gasoline. It was also very easy to make and mold into shape. Renamed "Neoprene," Dupont's synthetic rubber went on sale in 1937. Along with other plastics and synthetic rubbers, it had a dramatic effect. Synthetics replaced natural rubber in everything from car tires to condoms.

An even more significant achievement was the development of nylon. First conceived by DuPont as an alternative to silk, nylon had many other uses. It was first sold as toothbrush bristles in 1938. DuPont also set up a plant to produce nylon stockings, and by March 1939, more than five thousand pairs had been sold. Nylon turned out to be one of the most important developments in industrial chemistry. In the twenty-first century it is used in thousands of products, from bicycle tires to waterproof clothing and kitchen utensils. And more than sixty years later, toothbrush bristles are still made from nylon.

❖ RUDIMENTARY GENETIC SCIENCE

In the 1930s, genetics research was at the forefront of the biological sciences. The main question of the time was: how does a fixed set of genes produce such a huge variety of differences in a species? Two schools of thought existed. The German biologist August Weismann (1834–1914) studied the idea that certain traits were dominant and others "recessive." Recessive traits would only come to the fore when dominant traits were absent. Hugo de Vries (1848–1935) took a different approach. He investigated gene mutation. But genetics research was slow until the 1950s, when microscopes were developed that were powerful enough to provide a closer look.

In the absence of sophisticated physical evidence about genetics, socially influenced theories about the biology of the human race persisted during the decade. The idea behind the science of eugenics is that the hereditary qualities of a species can be improved through selective breeding. The idea that certain races were superior to others had a strong following in the United States in the 1930s, as did it in Germany during the same time period. Members of the eugenics movement, which was more political and social than scientific in nature, argued that "inferior" human races should be prevented from reproducing in order to control their numbers. Eugenicists believed that pure racial stock could be "contaminated" by inferior racial stock. Many states had laws against interracial marriage in an effort to prevent the birth of racially "mixed" children. Twenty-seven states had laws making it legal for "inferior" people to be sterilized to prevent them having children. The law was mostly applied to those in mental hospitals and prisons. In 1934 an article in the *Scientific American* argued that the case for population control had not been proved. But it also called one-fifth of the U.S. population "surplus," fueling eugenicists' arguments that society could not afford to support "inferior" people who could not support or care for themselves.

The American Eugenics Society (AES) had been founded in 1926. It reached its peak membership in 1930, with about 1,250 members. American eugenicists and sterilization laws were praised by Nazi Germany during the early years of the decade. In return, some white Americans believed that the shadowy Nazi practice of sterilizing Jews could provide an acceptable model for dealing with the African American population in the United States. By the mid-1930s, the eugenics movement was declining in political favor. The AES began to distance itself from the Nazis when news of the mass murder of Jews came to light late in the decade. By then the term

Many more men than women studied for science degrees in the 1930s. But increasing numbers of women were choosing science as a career. In 1938 a survey recorded 1,726 women working as professional scientists. Zoology, psychology, and botany were their preferred fields, with only eight working as engineers. Even so, the 1930s saw a 320 percent rise in the number of female scientists. Most of those counted would have held Ph.D.s, so many more women must have studied science at lower levels.

"eugenics" was associated with brutality and violence. As genetics research developed over the next two decades and beyond, many of the myths of the eugenics movement were exposed as having no basis in scientific evidence.

❖ EARTHLY STUDIES

In the 1930s differing theories about Earth's history highlighted the field of earth sciences. In 1912, German geologist Alfred Wegener (1880–1930) had proposed the idea that the continents had once been joined together. Wegener suggested that the continents were riding on huge tectonic plates that had drifted apart over the years. Evidence for his idea was found in the 1930s. Rock formations in South America and South Africa suggested that the two continents had once been linked, and the remains of similar prehistoric animals on both sides of the Atlantic also supported his idea. But despite the growing body of evidence, many scientists in the 1930s still opposed the idea of continental drift.

The movement of the earth intrigued other scientists in different ways. In 1935 Charles Richter (1900–1985) and Beno Gutenberg (1889–1960) developed a scale for measuring the strength of earthquakes. Working at the California Institute of Technology in Pasadena, Richter and Gutenberg used machines known as seismographs to measure vibrations and plot them on a graph. The scale measures the distances of a graphed line from the centerline. Although seismologists began to use the scale in the 1930s to evaluate earthquake strength, it was another twenty years before the scale was recognized or understood by the general public. Richter never used the term "Richter Scale," as it is known today, because he considered Gutenberg to be equally responsible for its development. Instead he called it "that confounded scale."

The study of Earth's weather, or meteorology, demonstrated great advances in the quantity and accuracy of information gathering during the 1930s. One of the key techniques for studying the weather in the 1930s was a device known as a radiosonde. Developed in Norway, a radiosonde is a radio transmitter suspended below a large, gas-filled balloon. It measures air pressure, wind speed, humidity, and temperature high up in the atmosphere. The information is transmitted back to base stations on the ground. From this information, 1930s meteorologists drew diagrams of weather patterns as they developed. These diagrams began to be collected on a daily basis in 1934. Other developments in the 1930s included "dynamic climatology." This was the study of air masses and weather fronts that tried to explain why rain clouds formed. In all, the world around us became much more understood thanks to the scientific advances of the 1930s.

❖ PHYSICS AND THE ATOMIC AGE

Like the other sciences, American physics benefited in the 1930s by scientists fleeing from dictatorships in Europe. Physicists from Europe and the United States worked together to make many important discoveries. These discoveries broadened our understanding of the world around us, but were not easily understood by many people. One of the most important inventions was Ernest Lawrence's (1901–1958) cyclotron, a machine that could separate particles from atoms. The cyclotron is the forebear of the huge, circular, particle accelerators used in the twenty-first century.

English physicist James Chadwick (1891–1974) discovered the neutron in 1932. Neutrons are particles inside atoms. Astrophysicist Carl David Anderson (1905–1991) identified the first antiparticle, known as the positron. Working with Seth Neddermayer (1907–1988) in 1937 Anderson also discovered the muon, another subatomic particle. Astronomer Edwin Powell Hubble (1889–1953) devised a method for working out the age of the universe and calculated that it was two billion years old. In 1939, the German physicist Hans Bethe (1906–) discovered that "stellar energy" detected in space was the result of nuclear reactions. From this he was able to calculate that the temperature at the center of the Sun is 18.5 million degrees Kelvin, or 333 million degrees Fahrenheit.

Research about subatomic particles led to some potentially devastating discoveries. German and Swedish scientists, Otto Hahn (1879–1968),

OPPOSITE PAGE
Charles Richter developed the Richter Scale, which measures the impact of earthquakes. Reproduced by permission of AP/Wide World Photos.

Lise Meitner (1878–1968), and Fritz Strassmann (1902–1980) found that by bombarding a form of uranium with neutrons, a huge amount of energy could be released. Hahn, Meitner, and Strassmann made their discovery in 1938, but the process of nuclear fission was first made public in

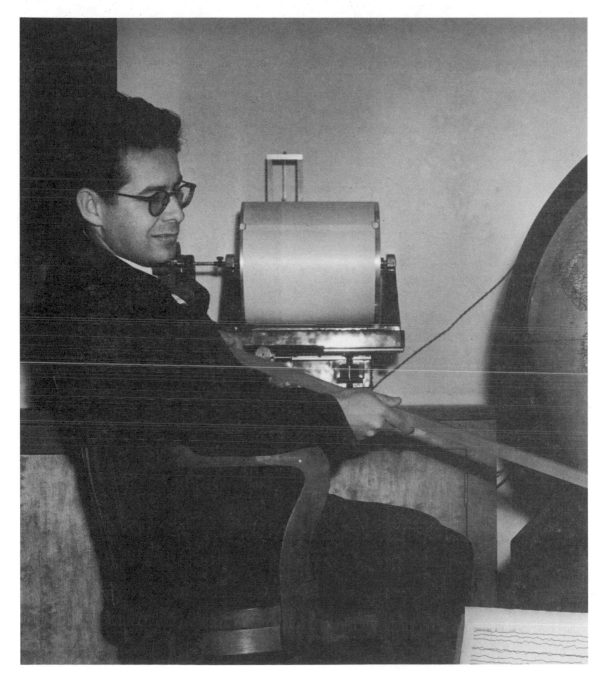

Scientific Terms

Antiparticle: A subatomic particle that corresponds to a similar subatomic particle with the opposite electric charge. For example, an antineutron is the antiparticle to the neutron.

Atom: The smallest particle of an element. Atoms are made up of protons, electrons, and neutrons. When the number of negative electrons and positive protons is the same, the atom is stable because they cancel each other out; the bigger the difference between the numbers of electrons and protons, the more unstable the atom will be.

Atomic number: The number of protons in the nucleus (core) of an atom; in the periodic table, the elements are arranged in order of their atomic number.

Electron: Part of an atom; Electrons have a negative charge.

Elements: Substances that cannot be broken down into other substances (examples are oxygen, hydrogen, and zinc); around ninety elements occur in nature; since the 1930s thirty more elements have been formed via nuclear reactions.

Genes: The units containing the information needed to make a living organism.

Isotope: An atom of an element that contains the same number of protons but different numbers of neutrons; isotopes are given a number after their name.

Periodic table: A table listing the chemical elements in order of their atomic number; it was devised in 1869 by Dmitri Mendeleyev (1834–1907).

Proton: Part of an atom; protons have a positive charge.

Synthesize: To make a substance artificially rather than collect it from nature; synthetic rubber is made in factories and natural rubber is collected from rubber trees.

1939 by Niels Bohr (1885–1962) at the American Physical Society in New York. What Bohr described in his address was the invention of the atomic bomb. Afraid that Nazi Germany would develop a useable atomic bomb first, American scientists persuaded Albert Einstein (1879–1955) to write President Franklin D. Roosevelt (1882–1945) requesting money for research into the bomb. Einstein was a well-known pacifist and

It was often difficult to find a clear signal on AM radio. Several inventors in the 1930s were looking for an alternative. The most significant of these was Edwin H. Armstrong (1890–1954). Between 1930 and 1933 he filed four patents for frequency modulation (FM). Working with RCA, Armstrong tested FM radio using the antenna on the top of the Empire State Building. Although FM was used by the military in during World War II, it wasn't until the 1950s that it took off commercially.

opposed to violence of all kinds, but he wrote the letter on August 2, 1939. The development of the atomic bomb would alter many people's ideas about war and life forever.

❖ TELEVISION'S FIRST TRANSMISSIONS

In 1931, several experiments were made with television broadcasting. Although the transmissions were available to the public, no private individuals had televisions to receive them. The Jenkins Television Corporation in New York City set up a five thousand–watt transmitter to broadcast television pictures, but no sound. The idea was that the WGBS radio station on Long Island would broadcast sound at exactly the same time. The receiver would pick up pictures and sound simultaneously. Not surprisingly, there were many problems. Televised pictures in 1931 were dark, shadowy, and unclear—far worse than the first movie pictures had been thirty years earlier.

By 1935, RCA (owner of NBC) was ready to spend a million dollars on TV broadcasting, using the Empire State Building as its transmitter. Two years later a new camera called an iconoscope dramatically improved picture quality. Experimental broadcasts were made, with technical standards improving all the time. In 1938, NBC was able to use a mobile TV unit to interview passersby on Rockefeller Plaza. On September 30, 1939, President Franklin D. Roosevelt (1882–1945) made the first ever televised address by an American president when he broadcast live from the New York World's Fair. But with early televisions costing a minimum of two hundred dollars, few Americans could afford to watch.

 *For More Information*

BOOKS

Asimov, Isaac. *How Did We Find Out About Atoms?* New York: Avon Books, 1982.

Asimov, Isaac. *How Did We Find Out About Vitamins?* New York: Walker, 1974.

Cohen, Daniel. *The Last Hundred Years, Household Technology.* New York: M. Evans, 1982.

Corn, Joseph J. *The Winged Gospel: America's Romance with Aviation, 1900–1950.* New York: Oxford University Press, 1983.

Dick, Harold, and Douglas Robinson. *The Golden Age of the Great Passenger Airships.* Washington, DC: Smithsonian Institution Press, 1985.

Dunar, Andrew J., and Dennis McBride. *Building Hoover Dam: An Oral History of the Great Depression.* Reno: University of Nevada Press, 2001.

Evernden, Margery. *The Experimenters: Twelve Great Chemists.* Greensboro, NC: Avisson Press, 2001.

Franck, Irene M., and David M. Brownstone. *Scientists and Technologists.* New York: Facts on File Publications, 1988.

Goddard, Stephen B. *Getting There: The Epic Struggle Between Road and Rail in the American Century.* New York: Basic Books, 1992.

Kevles, Daniel J. *The Physicists: The History of a Scientific Community in Modern America.* New York: Knopf, 1978.

McGowen, Tom. *Chemistry: The Birth of a Science.* New York: F. Watts, 1989.

McPherson, Stephanie Sammartino. *TV's Forgotten Hero: The Story of Philo Farnsworth.* Minneapolis: Carolrhoda Books, 1996.

Parker, Steve. *1920–40: Atoms to Automation.* Milwaukee, WI: Gareth Stevens Pub., 2001.

Richter, C. F. *Elementary Seismology.* San Francisco: Freeman, 1958.

Schafer, Mike. *Streamliner Memories.* Osceola, WI: MBI Pub., 1999.

Snedden, Robert. *The History of Genetics.* New York: Thomson Learning, 1995.

Spangenburg, Ray, and Diane K. Moser. *The Story of America's Bridges.* New York: Facts on File, 1991.

Stern, Ellen, and Emily Gwathmey. *Once Upon a Telephone: An Illustrated Social History.* New York: Harcourt Brace, 1994.

Stevens, J. E. *Hoover Dam: An American Adventure.* Norman: University of Oklahoma Press, 1988.

Stille, Darlene R. *Extraordinary Women Scientists.* Chicago: Children's Press, 1995.

Stwertka, Albert, and Eve Stwertka. *Physics: From Newton to the Big Bang.* New York: F. Watts, 1986.

Walters, Brian. *The Illustrated History of Air Travel.* New York: Marshall Cavendish, 1979.

Yount, Lisa. *Genetics and Genetic Engineering.* New York: Facts on File, 1997.

PERIODICALS

Hugh, F. D. "The Scientific American Digest." *Scientific American,* 144 (May 1931): p. 350.

Landman, J. H. "Race Betterment by Human Sterilization." *Scientific American,* 150 (June 1934): pp. 292–295.

WEB SITES

American Eugenics Society Scrapbook. http://www.amphilsoc.org/library/exhibits/treasures/aes.htm (accessed July 23, 2002).

American Institute of Physics: Center for History of Physics. http://www.aip.org/history/ (accessed July 23, 2002).

The Atomic Century. http://www.dpi.anl.gov/dpi2/timelines/1930s.htm (accessed July 23, 2002)

Earthquake Hazards Program: Science of Seismology. http://earthquake.usgs.gov/4kids//science.html (accessed July 23, 2002).

chapter eight *Sports*

1930: **May 17** Gallant Fox wins the Kentucky Derby, ridden by Earl Sande. The horse goes on to win almost every major race in the season.

1930: **September 18** The yacht *Enterprise* wins the seventy-ninth consecutive U.S. victory in the Americas Cup. It is the fifth time that Sir Thomas Lipton of England has been defeated by the Americans.

1930: **September 27** In golf, Bobby Jones completes his Grand Slam at the Merion Cricket Club in Ardmore, Pennsylvania.

1931: The Baseball Writers' Association of America awards its first Most Valuable Player (MVP) award to Frankie Frisch of the St. Louis Cardinals.

1931: **May 13** The United States beats France in boxing's first Golden Gloves competition.

1932: **February 4–13** The Winter Olympic Games take place at Lake Placid, New York.

1932: **June 2** A twenty-two pound, four-ounce largemouth bass is caught at Montgomery Lake, Georgia. This remains an International Game Fish Association (IFGA) All-Tackle world record.

1932: **June 22** In a tedious fight, Jack Sharkey takes the heavyweight boxing title from Max Schmeling.

1932: **July 30** The Summer Olympics opens in California. The next day American athletes set five Olympic track-and-field records in one day.

1932: **September 30** Lou Gehrig and Babe Ruth hit two home runs each in the third game of the Yankees-Cubs World Series. Ruth's second is his famous "called shot," in which Ruth pointed to the spot where he would hit a home run.

1933: **May 6** Broker's Tip wins the fifty-ninth Kentucky Derby.

1933: **August** The Negro League plays its East-West All-Star Games, watched by 50,000 fans at Comiskey Park in Chicago.

1933: **October 7** The Washington Senators lose to the New York Giants in what will be their last World Series game. The Giants take the series 4-1.

1934: The Augusta National in Georgia becomes the official course of the Masters Tournament.

1934: **August 31** At Soldier Field in Chicago, the first all-star football game is played between the Collegiate All-Americans and the Chicago Bears. The game ends in a scoreless tie.

1934: **October 9** The St. Louis Cardinals, known as the "Gashouse Gang," win the World Series against Detroit. A riot almost breaks out in the seventh game, and Joe Medwick is ordered out of the game.

1935: May 24 The Cincinnati Reds host the first major-league baseball night game, against Philadelphia. President Roosevelt presses a button in the White House to switch on the lights.

1935: May 25 At the Amateur Athletic Union track meet in Ann Arbor, Michigan, Jesse Owens breaks five world records and ties another in one afternoon.

1935: July 6 Helen Wills Moody wins her seventh Wimbledon tennis title against Helen Jacobs 6-3, 3-6, 7-5.

1935: September 3 At Bonneville Salt Flats in Utah, Malcolm Campbell's Bluebird automobile exceeds 300 miles per hour.

1936: February 8 The NFL holds its first college player draft. Jay Berwanger, winner of the first Heisman Trophy while playing for the University of Chicago, is the first pick. He decides not to turn professional.

1936: June 19 Max Schmeling knocks out heavyweight boxer Joe Louis, ending Louis's unbeaten run.

1936: August 2–9 Jesse Owens wins four gold medals at the Berlin Olympics.

1937: June 22 Joe Louis begins his long reign as heavyweight champion when he knocks out Jim Braddock at Comiskey Park, Chicago.

1937: July 20 Wimbledon champion Don Budge leads the U.S. Davis Cup team to victory for the first time since 1926.

1938: June 23 Joe Louis settles the score against Max Schmeling by knocking him out in the first round at Yankee Stadium in New York.

1938: August 17 Henry Armstrong becomes the first man to hold three boxing titles at the same time when he wins the lightweight crown. He also held the welterweight and featherweight titles.

1938: September 24 Don Budge becomes the first player to win all four major tennis titles in the same year.

1939: Little League baseball begins in Williamsport, Pennsylvania.

1939: May 2 Baseball star Lou Gehrig ends his fifteen-year consecutive game streak when he withdraws from the New York Yankees' starting lineup.

1939: October 8 The Yankees win their fourth straight World Series, defeating the Cincinnati Reds in four straight games.

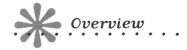

Overview

The year 1930 marked a dramatic change in American sports. The retirement of golfer Bobby Jones in that year signaled the end of a period when almost every sport had a single superstar. Throughout the 1930s, only Joe Louis dominated his sport as others had done in the so-called "golden age" of sports in the 1920s.

Like everything else in the United States, sports were deeply affected by the economic troubles known as the Great Depression. Many baseball and football franchises struggled to make a profit on gate receipts. Attendance at baseball games fell sharply in the 1930s, leaving little money for park renovations and forcing ballplayers' salaries down. Those who held out for more money, such as Joe DiMaggio in 1938, were publicly scorned. National Football League (NFL) teams lost money, and several withdrew from the league. In boxing, gate receipts had long exceeded the one million dollar mark for popular bouts. But in 1930 the Jack Sharkey-Max Schmeling fight failed to reach that mark. However, the Depression did increase participation in recreational sports, as many unemployed people found themselves with time on their hands.

As revenues fell, sports promoters and athletes looked for other ways to make money. Sports became more commercialized, and a debate raged about whether athletes should be amateur or professional. Many amateur athletes took to endorsing products or held paying jobs while they played for college teams. Sports journalists including Paul Gallico frowned on such promotions as night baseball and all-star baseball and football games. Some argued for a return to the "purity" of amateur sports.

The widening popularity of radio also made an impact on sports. Boxing matches, the Wimbledon tennis championship from England, and Army-Navy football games could all be heard live, via radio, across America. The 1932 Winter Olympics at Lake Placid, New York, proved a major draw for radio listeners. Sports sponsorship became an important form of advertising. In 1934 baseball commissioner Kenesaw Mountain Landis sold the rights to the baseball World Series for $100,000 to Ford Motors. Soon other major corporations were paying big money to promote their products during sports broadcasts. It was the beginning of a permanent link between big business and sports.

The entertainment industry also made an impact on sports in the 1930s. Aside from endorsements, radio announcing, and prize money, many athletes turned to Hollywood to make a living. In 1930, Olympic swimmer Johnny Weissmuller screentested for the role of "Tarzan, King of the Jungle." He is now better known for his screen performances than for his five Olympic gold medals and sixty-seven swimming records. Other athletes who broke into movies are tennis player Bill Tilden, figure skater Sonje Henie, and swimmer Buster Crabbe.

In many ways sports were ahead of other areas of American life in recognizing the achievements of African Americans. In the 1930s, colleges moved toward desegregation (ending the separation of the races) in track and field and in football. Black track star Jesse Owens and boxer Joe Louis became national heroes. Black athletes did a great deal to raise awareness of racial prejudice. But in the 1930s there was still a separate Negro League in baseball, while the NFL, which had accepted blacks until 1933, was all white from then until 1946.

The 1930s also saw the collapse of many of the taboos surrounding female athletes. The first women's gymnastics championships were held in 1931. In 1939 the first women's bicycling championship took place. But it was Mildred "Babe" Didrikson who did the most to raise the profile of women in American sports. Of the 634 amateur athletic competitions she entered in the 1920s and 1930s, she won in 632. She was part of a losing basketball team once and was disqualified from a high-jump contest where she appeared to set a world record.

Technology began to influence sport as never before. Britain's Malcolm Campbell repeatedly broke his own land speed records in his automobile, Bluebird, while in 1932 a 2,200 horsepower boat managed a record 101.351 miles per hour (mph). Two weeks later another boat managed 103.4 mph. In the Indianapolis 500 a diesel-powered car averaged 86.17 mph, finishing in thirteenth place without having to make a refueling stop. The photofinish camera made an appearance in 1936, and in 1937 underwater cameras decided the result of swimming contests.

The 1936 Olympics in Berlin were used by the German Nazi Party to try to demonstrate the superiority of German athletes. Germany won the most medals, but the games were dominated by stunning performances by black American athletes such as Jesse Owens. The 1938 Joe Louis-Max Schmeling fight became a "freedom versus fascism" grudge match. Louis emerged the victor.

Mildred "Babe" Didrikson (1911–1956) Mildred "Babe" Didrikson is generally thought to be the greatest female athlete who ever lived. One sportswriter said that short of winning the Kentucky Derby, there was nothing she couldn't do. She could hit home runs, score baskets, and was a record-breaking javelin thrower and hurdler. She was amateur and professional champion in many sports, including golf, and was named American Woman Athlete of the year in 1932. She died of cancer at the age of 54. *Photo reproduced by permission of the Corbis Corporation.*

Lou Gehrig (1903–1941) Known as "The Iron Horse" because of his willingness to play through injuries, Lou Gehrig was the New York Yankees' star player of the 1930s. At the end of his career he had played 2,130 consecutive games, with a batting average of .340, including 493 home runs. In 1932, he hit four home runs in one game. His consecutive streak of games began on May 31, 1925, and ended on May 2, 1939. On that day he announced to the crowd at the Yankee Stadium that he had a rare muscle disease. He died on June 2, 1941. *Photo reproduced by permission of Archive Photos, Inc.*

Helen Wills Moody (1905–1998) Between 1923 and 1938 tennis star Helen Wills Moody won eight Wimbledon titles, a record that stood until 1990. She also won seven U.S. National titles and four French titles. Although the press described her as refined and pleasant, Moody was in fact a ruthless champion. In the late 1930s, dogged by injuries and past her prime, Moody managed to win several tournaments on determination alone. In 1935, at Wimbledon, she came from down 5-2 at match point against Helen Jacobs (1908–1997) to record one of the greatest comebacks of all time. *Photo reproduced by permission of the Corbis Corporation.*

Bronko Nagurski (1908–1990) As the Chicago Bears' running back, Bronko Nagurski acquired a reputation for being unstoppable. His coach said the only way to stop him was to shoot him. He blocked punts and dragged players behind him for many yards. His formidable strength inspired stories of him pulling fenders off cars and knocking down walls. He was probably more intimidating than any player before his time. Retiring in 1937, Nagurski concentrated on professional wrestling, but he returned to football in 1943, playing for the Bears as a tackle until World War II (1938–45) ended. *Photo reproduced by permission of the Corbis Corporation.*

Jesse Owens (1913–1980) Jesse Owens's talent as a sprinter emerged at an early age. He matched the world record of 9.4 seconds for the 100-yard dash in 1932 at the age of nineteen. No colleges would take him, however, until Ohio State recognized his ability. Even so, Owens had to work as an elevator attendant to pay his way. Owens became an international star at the 1936 Berlin Olympics, winning the long jump and the 100-meter and 200-meter races and running as a member of the winning 400-meter relay team. Owens was known as the "colored runner" throughout his career, but he is remembered as the finest runner of his generation. *Photo reproduced by permission of Fisk University Library.*

Satchel Paige (1906–1982) Satchel Paige was the greatest pitcher of the 1930s and a huge box-office draw throughout the decade. Yet racial discrimination kept Paige out of the major leagues until 1948. In 1932 he joined the Pittsburgh Crawfords, the best black team of the period, and was well-known for his "Bee Ball." He joined the (white) Cleveland Indians in 1948, making the all-star team at the age of forty-six and pitched three innings for the Kansas City A's in 1965. He was elected to baseball's Hall of Fame in 1971. *Photo reproduced by permission of AP/Wide World Photos.*

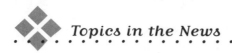

Topics in the News

❖ NO MORE B'RER RABBIT BALL: EVEN BASEBALL STRUGGLES

The spectacular baseball feats of the 1920s continued into the first year of the new decade. In 1930 National League batters averaged more than .300 in hitting and slugged nearly 900 home runs. The league was led by Bill Terry (1898–1989) of the Giants, who hit more than .400. Batting was less spectacular in the American League, but the New York Yankees and the Philadelphia Athletics matched National League averages. Sportswriter Ring Lardner (1885–1933) described the big hitting as "B'rer Rabbit Ball."

Despite the excitement of such home run spectacles, fans began to drift away from the sport known as the national pastime as the Depression deepened. In 1930, 10.1 million fans attended baseball games. By 1932 that figure had dropped to 8.1 million, and by 1933, there were only 6.3 million paying fans. Players' salaries fell as a result, with weaker clubs selling off talent to stay afloat. The 1930s saw the rise of the farm system. Richer clubs could afford to hire a great many young players, developing their talents in the lower leagues. They could unload surplus players or rent out ballparks to Negro League clubs. Radio eased the pressure on baseball clubs by allowing them to take in money from advertisers and broadcast sponsors. But only an improvement in the economy brought fans back to the ballparks.

The St. Louis Cardinals was the most colorful team of the mid-1930s. The filthy uniforms and tough reputation of the team's players earned them the nickname "The Gashouse Gang." Using older players like Pepper Martin (1904–1965) and young stars like Dizzy Dean (1911–1974), who won thirty games and saved seven, the Cardinals put together legendary season in 1934 and won the World Series by defeating Detroit in a dramatic seven-game series. In game five of the World Series, Dean was knocked out. Popular myth recalls a newspaper headline: "X-RAYS OF DEAN'S HEAD SHOW NOTHING."

The New York Yankees, however, was the dominant team of the decade. The team won four consecutive world championships between 1936 and 1939. The star player in the early 1930s was Babe Ruth (1895–1948). Ruth quit the Yankees in 1934, leaving the spotlight to Lou Gehrig (1903–1941), one of the most famous players of all time. By 1936 the full-time centerfielder was Joe DiMaggio (1914–1999), then aged twenty-one. Their excellent farm system meant that the Yankees ended the decade in all-conquering form.

Baseball player Bill Terry was the National League's most valuable player in 1930. He was the last National League player to hit over .400.
Reproduced by permission of AP/Wide World Photos.

Although the Depression had an impact on professional baseball, as America's favorite sport baseball was in no danger of going bankrupt. The Depression, however, nearly put an end to organized black baseball. (In the 1930s, professional baseball remained segregated, with black players barred from playing in the major leagues.) Despite financial problems, the Negro National League (NNL) was more exciting than ever. Many baseball immortals played in the NNL. The Pittsburgh Crawfords, for example, included Satchel Paige (1907–1982), Cool Papa Bell (1903–1991), and Judy Johnson (1899–1989).

❖ **BASKETBALL ADAPTS AND SURVIVES**

The American Basketball League (ABL) collapsed during the Depression, and the college game became the dominant form of basketball in the

1930s. College doubleheaders, played at Madison Square Garden, were a big draw. Promoted by Ned Irish (1905–1982), the first games took place on December 29, 1934, attracting a crowd of more than 16,000. The game sped up when the center jump after every basket was eliminated. Semipro leagues also did well, with company teams taking on college players after graduation. The ABL re-formed in 1933, and the National Basketball League (NBL) formed in 1937 from thirteen Midwest Industrial League teams. The NBL recruited college players and based itself on college rules. It was the basis for the Basketball Association of America, founded in 1949–50. Still, in the 1930s collegiate and company teams dominated the sport.

Among the few professional teams that survived the Depression were the Boston Celtics and the Brooklyn Visitations. The original Celtics had won around 90 percent of their games in the 1920s, and a new squad formed in 1931. Abe Saperstein's (1903–1966) Globetrotters were called "Harlem" because of the all-black squad, but were based in Chicago. In the 1930s they were a match for any other professional team.

The top professional basketball teams of the 1930s were the New York Rens and the Sphas (named for the South Philadelphia Hebrew Association). Based at the Renaissance Ballroom in Harlem, the all-black Rens had only seven players. Yet they were the best team between 1932 and 1936, with a record of 473-49. Their best winning streak was eighty-eight games in a row. The Rens were famous for their stamina, never calling time-outs themselves. As well as six-footers, the Rens' best lineup included Fats Jenkins (1898–1968), who was only five feet six inches tall. The other top team of the decade was the Sphas. Coach Eddie Gottlieb (1898–1979) led them to seven titles in thirteen years. The Broadwood Hotel, where they played, held dances after the games.

❖ BOXING: AMERICA'S SECOND SPORT

In the 1930s, boxing was the second most popular sport after baseball. Even in the depths of the Depression, fans would find the money to see their heroes fight. Radio cut into ringside profits, but tickets for the big fights still sold out quickly. Stars such as Joe Louis (1914–1981) became national heroes. A big part of the popularity of boxing was the gambling that went with it.

German Max Schmeling (1905–) took the heavyweight title in 1930 after Jack Sharkey (1902–1994) seemed to throw a below-the-belt punch. After Sharkey regained the title on points in 1932, sportswriters said that Schmeling had won the title lying down and lost it standing up. Italian Primo Carnera (1906–1967) became champion in 1933 after a series of fixed fights. But by 1934 the title was legitimately in the hands of Max Baer

(1909–1959). African American boxer Joe Louis and Schmeling eventually met in the ring for the first time in June 1936. Schmeling knocked out the American in twelve rounds. Their second meeting took place at Yankee Stadium on June 23, 1938. By that time Louis had been champion for a year. The grudge match was more than just a fight for a boxing title: Schmeling had joined the German Nazi Party, while Louis had come to symbolize freedom and democracy. Schmeling went down for the third and last time on two minutes and forty seconds. He had managed to throw just two punches. Louis won the title, and for the next twelve years he dominated the sport. He gave up the title when he retired in 1949.

Although the heavyweight title drew the most attention, there was dramatic action in lighter divisions as well. Light heavyweights such as John Henry Lewis (1914–1974) gave up their titles to compete with heavyweight stars. Billy Conn (1917–1993), one of the best light heavyweights of the 1930s, went on to fight Joe Louis (1914–1981), almost relieving him of the heavyweight title in 1941. Meanwhile the middleweight division was in turmoil. Seven fighters had a claim to the suspect National Boxing Association (NBA) title between 1933 and 1939. The New York boxing title was held for most of the decade by Fred Apostoli (1914–1973). Jimmy McLarnin (1907–) and former lightweight Barney Ross (1907–1967) shook up the welterweight division in the 1930s. McLarnin had killed a boxer named Pancho Villa (1901–1925) in a match in 1925, and his hard-hitting style won him the welterweight crown in 1933. Ross took the title in 1934, only to have McLarnin beat him the following year. Ross regained the title from McLarnin in 1935 and held onto it until 1938. Among the lightweights, Tony Canzoneri, Lou Ambers, Henry Armstrong, and Ross exchanged the title over the course of the decade.

❖ FOOTBALL: A GAME IN NEED OF CHANGE

After a Yale University player was killed in 1931, reformers called for changes to college football. The college game had become semiprofessional and was corrupted by press coverage and money. In fact, college football began to reform itself. The University of Chicago withdrew funding from its football program and dropped it altogether in 1939. In 1937, Notre Dame decided that the University of Pittsburgh was a professional team and dropped it from the schedule. This forced Pitt to reform. It stopped paying players and scaled down its training program. Pittsburgh coach Jock Sutherland (1889–1948) left the college game and moved to the openly professional National Football League (NFL).

For most fans in the 1930s the college game was the only football that really counted. In 1934 the *Chicago Tribune's* Arch Ward (1896–1955) set

The first televised sports event was the English Derby in 1931. But 1939 saw several live televised sports broadcasts.

May 17	The first college baseball game, between Princeton and Columbia.
June 1	First heavyweight boxing match, between Lou Nova and Max Baer.
August 9	First tennis match, between the Eastern Grass Court Championships.
September 26	First major league baseball game, between the Dodgers and the Reds.
September 30	First college football game, between Fordham and Wyoming.

up the first all-star game, where the best college players would play the NFL's Chicago Bears. That first all-star game ended in a 0-0 tie. Other post-season bowl games began in the 1930s, including the Orange Bowl (1935), the Sugar Bowl (1935), the Sun Bowl (1936), the Cotton Bowl (1937), and the Blue-Gray Game (1938), not to mention the long forgotten Ice Bowl, Rhumba Bowl, and Tobacco Bowl.

Professional football, which began in the 1920s, continued to develop in the 1930s. In 1930, the NFL champion was the team with the best record. But in 1933 a championship game decided the title between Eastern and Western division winners. The first Pro Bowl took place in 1938 between all-stars from throughout the league and NFL champions the New York Giants. The NFL began to make play more offensive. A rule change allowed the ball to be thrown as far forward as possible, rather than just five yards behind the defensive line. Meanwhile the single wing gave way to the T-formation. Sid Luckman (1916–1998) of the Chicago Bears became the NFL's first T-formation quarterback in 1939.

In both college and pro football, the game became more open and exciting. In the 1920s there were a limited number of plays, few passes, and players played both offense and defense. Sammy Baugh (1914–), the quarterback at Texas Christian University, proved that the pass attack could work in the mid-1930s. He shocked a superior Santa Clara team and beat Marquette in the Cotton Bowl in 1936. In 1937, his rookie year in the NFL, Baugh led the Washington Redskins to the Eastern Division title. He broke all the passing records up to that time. Don Hutson (1913–1997), who played with the Green Bay Packers from 1935 to 1945, made the wide receiver a crucial part of the game. For speed and catching ability, nobody could match Hutson.

❖ FOR GOLF, BETTER CLUBS AND BETTER COURSES

Many private country clubs lost money and closed during the Depression, but the number of golf courses in the nation actually grew during the decade. Through the Works Progress Administration (WPA; a government spending program), the federal government built nearly two hundred new public courses in the 1930s. The new courses were well designed and kept in better shape than previous public courses had been. The Augusta National opened at Augusta, Georgia, in 1934 and became the home of the Masters tournament. Miniature golf was also popular in the 1930s. In 1930 Chattanooga, Tennessee, hosted the first national open miniature golf championship, but by 1940 the miniature golf craze was over.

The golfing sensation of the 1920s, Bobby Jones (1902–1971), retired in 1930 after winning the Grand Slam. Fans were looking for someone to replace him. Gene Sarazen (1901–1999) came from behind to win the U.S. Open in 1932 at the age of twenty. But Sarazen's long career was also inconsistent. Lawson Little Jr. (1910–1968), who won the U.S. and British Open events in both 1934 and 1935, was not the fans' favorite. Similarly Ralph Guldahl (1912–1987), who won the U.S. Open in 1937 and 1938, always seemed cold and distant. Only when Sam Snead (1912–2002) and Byron Nelson (1912–) appeared at the end of the decade did any golfers gain public attention and affection that rivalled that of Bobby Jones.

The Professional Golfers' Association (PGA) held thirty-three tournaments in 1933. The total winnings for the whole season came to $135,000. Johnny Revolta (1911–1991) won $10,000 that year. Two hundred other pros split the rest. Amateurs competed with, and often beat, the pros. Women golfers, who were all amateur, could hit in the low 70s. Virginia Van Wie (1909–1997) won three consecutive amateur titles between 1932 and 1934.

❖ A DAY AT THE RACES

Horse racing had always been popular in the United States, but in the 1920s and 1930s it vied with boxing to be the second most popular sport after baseball. The Marx Brothers' film *A Day at the Races* (1937) and stories of Damon Runyon (1884–1946) are evidence that horse racing had captured the popular imagination. The popularity of the horse racing was also boosted in the 1930s when boxing was rocked by a series of fight-fixing rumors.

The Triple Crown (a trio of victories in the three major horse races: the Kentucky Derby, the Preakness Stakes, and the Belmont Stakes) of 1930 went to Gallant Fox, a three-year-old ridden by Earl Sande (1898–1968). In the Belmont Stakes he faced tough competition from Whichone. The Dwyer and the Arlington Classic also went to Gallant Fox, and by the end of the season he was the top-winning racehorse. He was finally beaten by Jim Dandy at the muddy Saratoga Springs track. There were two more Triple Crown winners during the decade: Omaha in 1935 and War Admiral in 1937.

One of the best-loved horses of the 1930s and beyond was Seabiscuit. When he first began racing in 1935, Seabiscuit was not considered much of a threat in any contest. Described unkindly as "phlegmatic," he was undersized and the wrong shape for a thoroughbred. When he took to the Pimlico track on November 1, 1938, he went up against War Admiral, 1937's Triple Crown winner. Seabiscuit was an outside bet at best. But Seabiscuit managed to pull out a full-length lead. In the home stretch War Admiral led by a nose until Seabiscuit broke away to win by three lengths. Sportswriters called it the race of the decade.

❖ HOCKEY: THE CANADIAN GAME

Ninety percent of hockey players in the 1930s were Canadian, but the decade saw the game grow more popular in the United States. National Hockey League (NHL) teams in Boston, New York, and Detroit all helped build the organized league. In 1928 the New York Rangers were the first American team to win the Stanley Cup, and they almost did it again in 1930. The Chicago Black Hawks won in 1934, thanks to playmaker Harold "Mush" March (1918–) and goaltender Charlie Gardiner (1904–1934). The Black Hawks won the Stanley Cup a second time in 1938.

Hockey rules changed in 1930 to allow forward passing in all zones. (From the 1933–1934 season only three players were allowed in the defensive zone.) But as the game became faster, it also became more violent. Unprotected heads were whacked with sticks, and fistfights were common. Goalie Clint Benedict (1894–1976) broke his nose three times and designed a protective leather mask. He rarely wore the mask, however, because he didn't want to be thought a coward.

As the 1930s went on, hockey franchises reduced in number from ten to seven. The schedule covered forty-eight games. Players became faster, more nimble skaters, and stick handling improved. Amateur hockey also became popular in the United States in the 1930s.

The biggest hockey star of the decade was Howie "Stratford Streak" Morenz (1902–1937). Playing for the Montreal Canadiens, Morenz won two consecutive Hart Trophies as the league's Most Valuable Player. In 1936 he was traded mid-season from Chicago to the New York Rangers. In decline, he returned to the Canadiens in 1937, only to be badly injured during a game. While hospitalized with a broken leg, Morenz suffered a nervous breakdown and died of heart failure at the age of thirty-four. Future Hall of Famers whose careers began in the 1930s include: Syl Apps, Frank Boucher, Eddie Shore, Earl Siebert, Babe Siebert, Art Coulter, Charlie Lonacher, Dave Schriner, Toe Blake, and Tiny Thompson.

❖ OLYMPIC GAMES RAISE SPIRITS, ANGER HITLER

The 1932 Winter and Summer Olympic Games helped raise the national spirit during the depths of the Depression. The Winter Games were held at Lake Placid, New York. Americans did well, winning six gold, three silver, and two bronze medals. For the first time in a Winter Games, the U.S. team won more medals than any other nation. Canada won the ice hockey gold medal for the fourth consecutive time.

The 1932 Summer Olympics took place in Los Angeles. Now considered the greatest woman athlete of all time, Mildred "Babe" Didrikson (1911–1956) broke records in the javelin and in the eighty-meter hurdles. She was bumped down to silver in the high jump after diving over the bar on her gold medal attempt. American women won half of the track and field medals on offer. American men also dominated. Eddie Tolan (1909–1967) beat fellow American Ralph Metcalfe (1910–1978) to set a 100-meter world record. In the pool, Clarence "Buster" Crabbe (1908–1983), later to star as Flash Gordon in the movies, won gold in the 400-meter freestyle.

The 1936 Winter Games, held at Garmisch Partenkirchen, Germany, saw few American successes. The lone gold medal went to the two-man bobsled. As Adolf Hitler's Nazi Party strengthened its grip on the country, political events overshadowed this low-key Winter Games. The Summer Games of 1936 have become famous for the way the Nazis used them for propaganda. By 1936, German Jews had been stripped of their citizenship and civil rights. Germany was building a war machine that would eventually engulf most of Europe. But having offered the Games to Germany in 1931, the Olympic committee allowed them to go ahead. Hitler decided to use the games to demonstrate the superiority of the Aryan (white) race. Many observers, including American swimmer Eleanor Holm (1913–), were charmed by high-ranking Nazis such as Hermann Goering (1893–1946).

But Hitler's plan to show the world his brilliant Aryan athletes achieved only mixed success. Black American athletes won eight gold, three silver, and two bronze medals in track and field. Sprinter Jesse Owens (1913–1980) won four golds. But although popular myth states that Hitler snubbed Owens, it was not the case. It was Cornelius Johnson (1913–1946), the high-jump gold medal winner, whom Hitler ignored on the podium. Germans won 101 of the medals, with the United States in second place with 57. Despite his distaste for the success of black athletes during the games, Hitler gained the sports field victory he wanted.

❖ THE END OF A GOLDEN AGE OF TENNIS

As in many other sports, 1930 marked the end of a golden age in tennis. American Bill Tilden (1893–1953) and French player Suzanne Lenglen (1899–1938) dominated the game in the 1920s. In the 1930s tennis increased in popularity, but disputes over amateur and professional status raged. By 1939 it was almost impossible to tell the difference between amateur and professional players. Many players turned professional to avoid falling foul of the rules governing amateur play.

Tennis had always been an upper middle-class game, and not much had changed by the 1930s. The United States Lawn Tennis Association (USLTA) worked to make tennis a game for everyone. Young people were encouraged to play by a Junior Davis Cup program for boys (1935), and a Junior Wightman Cup for girls (1938). African Americans, however, were not welcome. They played under the American Tennis Association (ATA).

The U.S., British, Australian, and French Open tennis tournaments dominated international tennis. American Donald Budge (1915–2000) won all four titles in 1938. His Grand Slam was all the more impressive since the ball had become harder and faster that year. Women's tennis changed too. As the international game became more demanding, women wore Bermuda shorts and other more athletic clothing. They served overhead, while Alice Marble (1913–1990) began the power-serve and volley game.

Since its primary paying audience was not badly hurt by the Depression, neither was the sport of tennis. Bill Tilden (1893–1953), Don Budge (1915–2000), and others drew huge crowds to their professional games at Forest Hills and Madison Square Garden. Helen Wills Moody (1905–1998) was nearing the end of her career when she won Wimbledon in 1935. Budge's five set match against Baron Gottfried von Cramm at the 1937 Wimbledon championship was one of the greatest of all time. Budge came back from being down 4-1 in the final set to win after seven match points. The United States also won the Davis Cup international team tournament that year for the first time in a decade.

Tennis player Helen Wills Moody won 31 major tennis titles and an Olympic gold medal in 1924. She was nearing the end of her career when she won Wimbledon in 1935. Reproduced by permission of Archive Photos, Inc.

❖ **INTEGRATION IN TRACK AND FIELD**

Of all sports, track and field was the most integrated in the 1930s. White colleges sought black athletes knowing they could not win without them. Jesse Owens (1913–1980) went to Ohio State University, Eddie Tolan (1909–1967) went to the University of Michigan, and Ralph Metcalfe (1910–1978) went to Marquette University. Blacks still suffered racism in colleges and at track meetings, but the success of Owens and others advanced the cause of African Americans in other sports.

Paavo Nurmi (1897–1973) of Finland dominated the popular mile race in the 1920s, but the 1930s belonged to Glenn Cunningham (1910–1988) and Bill Bonthron (1912–1983). In the Princeton Invitation Meet of that year, Cunningham ran 4:06.7 for a mile. Races between Cunningham and Bonthron drew record crowds. "Galloping Glenn" was one of the best-known American athletes of the decade.

For More Information

BOOKS

Aaseng, Nathan. *Women Olympic Champions*. San Diego, CA: Lucent Books, 2001.

Anderson, Dave. *The Story of Basketball*. New York: W. Morrow, 1997.

Bacho, Peter. *Boxing in Black and White*. New York: H. Holt and Co., 1999.

Bak, Richard. *Joe Louis: The Great Black Hope*. New York: Da Capo Press, 1998.

Bayne, Bijan C. *Sky Kings: Black Pioneers of Professional Basketball*. New York: F. Watts, 1997.

Camper, Erich. *Encyclopedia of the Olympic Games*. New York: McGraw Hill, 1972.

Christopher, Matt. *Great Moments in Baseball History*. Boston: Little, Brown, 1996.

Collins, Ace, and John Hillman. *Blackball Superstars: Legendary Players of the Negro Baseball Leagues*. Greensboro, NC: Avisson Press, 1999.

Cooper, Michael L. *Playing America's Game: The Story of Negro League Baseball*. New York: Lodestar Books, 1993.

Duke, Jacqueline, ed. *Thoroughbred Champions: Top 100 Racehorses of the Twentieth Century*. Lexington, KY: The Blood-Horse, Inc., 1999.

Dunnahoo, Terry Janson, and Herma Silverstein. *Baseball Hall of Fame*. New York: Maxwell Macmillan International, 1994.

Gilbert, Thomas. *The Good Old Days: Baseball in the 1930s*. New York: F. Watts, 1996.

Greenspan, Bud. *100 Greatest Moments in Olympic History*. Los Angeles: General Publishing Group, 1995.

Grimsley, Will. *Tennis: It's History, People, and Events*. Englewood Cliffs, NJ: Prentice-Hall. 1971.

Gross, John, and the editors of *Golf Magazine*. *The Encyclopedia of Golf*. New York: Harper and Row, 1979.

Hillenbrand, Lauren. *Seabiscuit: An American Legend*. New York: Random House, 2001.

Hollander, Zander. *Home Run: Baseball's Greatest Hits and Hitters*. New York: Random House, 1984.

Hollander, Zander, and Ed Bock, eds. *The Complete Encyclopedia of Hockey*. Englewood Cliffs, NJ: Prentice-Hall, 1974.

Italia, Bob. *100 Unforgettable Moments in Pro Tennis*. Edina, MN: Abdo & Daughters, 1996.

Kahn, Roger. *Games We Used to Play*. New York: Tickner and Fields, 1992.

Blum, Stella. *Everyday Fashions of the Thirties as Pictured in Sears Catalogs.* New York: Dover, 1986.

Booker, Christopher B. *African-Americans and the Presidency: A History of Broken Promises.* New York: Franklin Watts, 2000.

Bowen, David J. *The Struggle Within: Race Relations in the United States.* New York: Grosset and Dunlap, 1972.

Brennan, Kristine. *The Stock Market Crash of 1929.* Philadelphia: Chelsea House Publishers, 2000.

Brinkley, Alan. *Voices of Protest: Huey Long, Father Coughlin, and the Great Depression.* New York: Knopf, 1982.

Bryan, Jenny. *The History of Health and Medicine.* Austin, TX: Raintree/Steck-Vaughn, 1996.

Burge, Michael C., and Don Nardo. *Vaccines: Preventing Disease.* San Diego, CA: Lucent Books, 1992.

Camper, Erich. *Encyclopedia of the Olympic Games.* New York: McGraw-Hill, 1972.

Carson, Richard Burns. *The Olympian Cars: The Great American Luxury Automobiles of the Twenties and Thirties.* New York: Knopf, 1976.

Christopher, Matt. *Great Moments in Baseball History.* Boston: Little, Brown, 1996.

Cobb, William H. *Radical Education in the Rural South: Commonwealth College 1923–1940.* Detroit: Wayne State University Press, 2000.

Cohen, Daniel. *The Last 100 Years: Medicine.* New York: M. Evans, 1981.

Collier, Christopher, and James Lincoln Collier. *Progressivism, the Great Depression, and the New Deal, 1901 to 1941.* New York: Benchmark Books/Marshall Cavendish, 2001.

Collins, Ace, and John Hillman. *Blackball Superstars: Legendary Players of the Negro Baseball Leagues.* Greensboro, NC: Avisson Press, 1999.

Constantino, Maria, Elane Feldman, and Valerie Cumming, eds. *Fashions of a Decade: The 1930s.* New York: Facts on File, 1992.

Cook, Chris, and David Waller, eds. *The Longman Handbook of Modern American History, 1763–1996.* New York: Longman, 1998.

Cooper, Michael L. *Playing America's Game: The Story of Negro League Baseball.* New York: Lodestar Books, 1993.

Corn, Joseph J. *The Winged Gospel: America's Romance with Aviation, 1900–1950.* New York: Oxford University Press, 1983.

Cowley, Malcolm. *Think Back on Us—A Contemporary Chronicle of the 1930s.* Southern Illinois University Press, 1967.

Cunningham, Robert, III, and Robert Cunningham Jr. *The Blues: A History of the Blue Cross and Blue Shield System.* DeKalb, IL: Northern Illinois University Press, 1997.

Devaney, John. *Franklin Delano Roosevelt, President.* New York: Walker and Co., 1987.

Dick, Harold, and Douglas Robinson. *The Golden Age of the Great Passenger Airships*. Washington, D.C.: Smithsonian Institution Press, 1985.

Dowswell, Paul. *Medicine*. Chicago: Heinemann Library, 2001.

Dreiser, Theodore. *Harlan Miners Speak*. New York: De Capo Books, 1933.

Dubinsky, David, and A. H. Raskin. *David Dubinsky: A Life with Labor*. New York: Simon and Schuster, 1977.

Duke, Jacqueline, ed. *Thoroughbred Champions: Top 100 Racehorses of the Twentieth Century*. Lexington, KY: The Blood-Horse, Inc., 1999.

Dunar, Andrew J., and Dennis McBride. *Building Hoover Dam: An Oral History of the Great Depression*. Reno: University of Nevada Press, 2001.

Dunnahoo, Terry Janson, and Herma Silverstein. *Baseball Hall of Fame*. New York: Maxwell Macmillan International, 1994.

Eaton, William Edward. *The American Federation of Teachers, 1916–1961: A History of the Movement*. Carbondale: Southern Illinois University Press, 1975.

Evernden, Margery. *The Experimenters: Twelve Great Chemists*. Greensboro, NC: Avisson Press, 2001.

Farrell, Jacqueline. *The Great Depression*. San Diego, CA: Lucent Books, 1996.

Feinstein, Stephen. *The 1930s: From the Great Depression to the Wizard of Oz*. New York: Enslow Publishers, 2001.

Franck, Irene M., and David M. Brownstone. *Scientists and Technologists*. New York: Facts on File Publications, 1988.

Freedman, Russell. *Eleanor Roosevelt: A Life of Discovery*. New York: Clarion Books, 1993.

Freedman, Russell. *Franklin Delano Roosevelt*. New York: Clarion Books, 1990.

Garza, Hedda. *Women in Medicine*. New York: Franklin Watts, 1994.

Gilbert, Thomas. *The Good Old Days: Baseball in the 1930s*. New York: Franklin Watts, 1996.

Glassman, Bruce. *The Crash of '29 and the New Deal*. Morristown, NJ: Silver Burdett Co., 1986.

Goddard, Stephen B. *Getting There: The Epic Struggle Between Road and Rail in the American Century*. New York: Basic Books, 1992.

Gottfried, Ted. *Alexander Fleming: Discoverer of Penicillin*. New York: Franklin Watts, 1997.

Goulart, Ron. *Comic Book Culture: An Illustrated History*. Portland, OR: Collector's Press, 2000.

Greenspan, Bud. *100 Greatest Moments in Olympic History*. Los Angeles: General Publishing Group, 1995.

Grimsley, Will. *Tennis: It's History, People, and Events*. Englewood Cliffs, NJ: Prentice-Hall. 1971.

Gruber, J. Richard. *Thomas Hart Benton and the American South*. Augusta, GA: Morris Museum of Art, 1998.

Guthrie, Woody. *Bound for Glory.* New York: New American Library, 1995.

Hamilton, Sue L. *John Dillinger.* Bloomington, IN: Abdo & Daughters, 1989.

Harris, Cyril M. *American Architecture: An Illustrated Encyclopedia.* New York: W. W. Norton, 1998.

Haskins, James. *Separate, but Not Equal: The Dream and the Struggle.* New York: Scholastic, 1998.

Hawes, Elizabeth. *Fashion Is Spinach.* New York: Random House, 1938.

Hillenbrand, Lauren. *Seabiscuit: An American Legend.* New York: Random House, 2001.

Holford, David M. *Herbert Hoover.* Springfield, NJ: Enslow, 1999.

Hollander, Zander. *Home Run: Baseball's Greatest Hits and Hitters.* New York: Random House, 1984.

Hollander, Zander, and Ed Bock, eds. *The Complete Encyclopedia of Hockey.* Englewood Cliffs, NJ: Prentice-Hall, 1974.

Howe, Irving, and B. J. Widick. *The UAW and Walter Reuther.* New York: De Capo Books, 1973.

Hunt, Marsha. *The Way We Wore: Styles of the 1930s and '40s and Our World Since Then.* Fallbrook, CA: Fallbrook, 1993.

Isaacs, Sally Senzell. *America in the Time of Franklin Delano Roosevelt: The Story of Our Nation from Coast to Coast, from 1929 to 1948.* Des Plaines, IL: Heinemann Library, 2000.

Italia, Bob. *100 Unforgettable Moments in Pro Tennis.* Edina, MN: Abdo & Daughters, 1996.

Jones, Constance. *Karen Horney.* New York: Chelsea House, 1989.

Joseph, Paul. *Herbert Hoover.* Minneapolis: Abdo & Daughters, 2001.

Kahn, Roger. *Games We Used to Play.* New York: Tickner and Fields, 1992.

Kevles, Daniel J. *The Physicists: The History of a Scientific Community in Modern America.* New York: Knopf, 1978.

Klehr, Harvey. *The Heyday of American Communism: The Depression Decade.* New York: Basic Books, 1984.

Landau, Elaine. *Tuberculosis.* New York: Franklin Watts, 1995.

Larsen, Rebecca. *Franklin D. Roosevelt: Man of Destiny.* New York: Franklin Watts, 1991.

Latham, Frank Brown. *FDR and the Supreme Court Fight, 1937: A President Tries to Reorganize the Federal Judiciary.* New York: Franklin Watts, 1972.

Lindop, Edmund. *Modern America: The Turbulent Thirties.* New York: Franklin Watts, 1970.

Lindsay, Paul. *Breaking the Bonds of Racism.* Homewood, IL: ETC Publications, 1974.

Liss, Howard. *They Changed the Game: Football's Great Coaches, Players, and Games.* Philadelphia: Lippincott, 1975.

Lucas, Eileen. *The Eighteenth and Twenty-First Amendments: Alcohol, Prohibition, and Repeal.* Springfield, NJ: Enslow Publishers, 1998.

Lusane, Clarence. *The Struggle for Equal Education.* New York: Franklin Watts, 1992.

Manchel, Frank. *The Talking Clowns: From Laurel and Hardy to the Marx Brothers.* New York: Franklin Watts, 1976.

Mank, Gregory William. *Women in Horror Films, 1930s.* Jefferson, NC: McFarland and Company, 1999.

Margolies, John. *Fun Along the Road: American Tourist Attractions.* Boston: Little Brown & Company, 1998.

Martin, Richard. *Jocks and Nerds: Men's Style in the Twentieth Century.* New York: Rizzoli, 1989.

Mazo, Joseph H. *Prime Movers: The Makers of Modern Dance in America.* New York: Morrow Quill Paperbacks, 1980.

McGowen, Tom. *Chemistry: The Birth of a Science.* New York: Franklin Watts, 1989.

McPherson, Stephanie Sammartino. *TV's Forgotten Hero: The Story of Philo Farnsworth.* Minneapolis: Carolrhoda Books, 1996.

Melton, J. Gordon. *American Religions: An Illustrated History.* Santa Barbara, CA: ABC-CLIO, 2000.

Meltzer, Milton. *Driven from the Land: The Story of the Dust Bowl.* New York: Benchmark Books, 2000.

Miller, Brandon Marie. *Just What the Doctor Ordered: The History of American Medicine.* Minneapolis, MN: Lerner Publications, 1997.

Moloney, James H. *Encyclopedia of American Cars, 1930–1942.* Glen Ellyn, IL: Crestline, 1977.

Nishi, Dennis. *Life During the Great Depression.* San Diego, CA: Lucent Books, 1998.

Oermann, Robert K. *A Century of Country: An Illustrated History of Country Music.* New York: TV Books, 1999.

Park, Marlene. *New Deal for Art: The Government Art Projects of the 1930s With Examples from New York City and State.* New York: Gallery Association of New York State, 1977.

Parker, Steve. *Medical Advances.* Austin, TX: Raintree/Steck-Vaughn, 1998.

Parker, Steve. *1920–40: Atoms to Automation.* Milwaukee, WI: Gareth Stevens Pub., 2001.

Pasachoff, Naomi E. *Frances Perkins: Champion of the New Deal.* Oxford: Oxford University Press Children's Books, 2000.

Peper, George. *The Story of Golf.* New York: TV Books, 1999.

Polikoff, Barbara Garland. *Herbert C. Hoover, 31st President of the United States.* Ada, OK: Garrett Educational Corp., 1990.

Pont, Sally. *Fields of Honor: The Golden Age of College Football and the Men Who Created It.* New York: Harcourt, 2001.

Press, Petra. *The 1930s.* San Diego, CA: Lucent, 1999.

Rensberger, Susan. *A Multicultural Portrait of the Great Depression.* Tarrytown, NY: Benchmark Books, 1996.

Richter, C. F. *Elementary Seismology.* San Francisco: Freeman, 1958.

Robinson, Max, and Jack Kramer, eds. *The Encyclopedia of Tennis: One Hundred Years of Great Players and Events.* New York: Viking, 1974.

Roesch, Roberta. *World's Fairs: Yesterday, Today, Tomorrow.* New York: John Day, 1964.

Ross, Stewart. *Causes and Consequences of the Great Depression.* Austin, TX: Raintree/Steck-Vaughn, 1998.

Royston, Angela. *100 Greatest Medical Discoveries.* Danbury, CT: Grolier Educational, 1997.

Ryan, Pat. *The Heavyweight Championship.* Mankato, MN: Creative Education, 1993.

Sayers, Janet. *Mothers of Psychoanalysis: Helen Deutsch, Karen Horney, Anna Freud, and Melanie Klein.* New York: W. W. Norton, 1993.

Schafer, Mike. *Streamliner Memories.* Osceola, WI: MBI Pub., 1999.

Schatz, Thomas. *The Genius of the System: Hollywood Filmmaking in the Studio Era.* New York: Pantheon, 1988.

Scheehan, Angela, ed. *The Marshall Cavendish Encyclopedia of Health.* New York: Marshall Cavendish, 1995.

Schmeling, Max, and George B. von der Lippe, trans. and ed. *Max Schmeling: An Autobiography.* Chicago, IL: Bonus Books, 1998.

Schraff, Anne E. *The Great Depression and the New Deal: America's Economic Collapse and Recovery.* New York: Franklin Watts, 1990.

Shaw, Arnold. *Let's Dance: Popular Music in the 1930s.* New York: Oxford University Press, 1998.

Sherrow, Victoria. *Hardship and Hope: America and the Great Depression.* New York: Twenty-First Century Books, 1997.

Sifakis, Carl. *The Encyclopedia of American Crime,* 2nd ed. New York: Facts on File, 2001.

Silverstein, Alvin, et al. *Polio.* Berkeley Heights, NJ: Enslow Publishers, 2001.

Smith, Wendy. *Real Life Drama: The Group Theatre and America 1931–1940.* New York: Knopf, 1990.

Snedden, Robert. *The History of Genetics.* New York: Thomson Learning, 1995.

Southern, Eileen. *The Music of Black Americans: A History.* New York: Norton, 1983.

Spangenburg, Ray, and Diane K. Moser. *The Story of America's Bridges.* New York: Facts on File, 1991.

Stein, R. Conrad. *The Story of the Great Depression.* Chicago: Children's Press, 1985.

Stern, Ellen, and Emily Gwathmey. *Once Upon a Telephone: An Illustrated Social History.* New York: Harcourt Brace, 1994.

Stevens, J. E. *Hoover Dam: An American Adventure.* Norman: University of Oklahoma Press, 1988.

Stewart, Mark. *Baseball: A History of the National Pastime.* New York: Franklin Watts, 1998.

Stewart, Mark. *Basketball: A History of Hoops.* New York: Franklin Watts, 1998.

Stewart, Mark. *Hockey: A History of the Fastest Game on Ice.* New York: Franklin Watts, 1998.

Stille, Darlene R. *Extraordinary Women of Medicine.* New York: Children's Press, 1997.

Stille, Darlene R. *Extraordinary Women Scientists.* Chicago: Children's Press, 1995.

Stockdale, Tom. *The Life and Times of Al Capone.* Philadelphia, PA: Chelsea House Publishers, 1997.

Stone, Lee Tanya. *The Great Depression and World War II.* Austin, TX: Raintree/Steck-Vaughn, 2001.

Struhel, John Warthen. *The History of American Classical Music.* New York: Facts on File, 1995.

Stwertka, Albert, and Eve Stwertka. *Physics: From Newton to the Big Bang.* New York: Franklin Watts, 1986.

Terkel, Studs. *Hard Times: An Oral History of the Great Depression.* New York: Random House, 1970.

Uschan, Michael V. *Golf.* San Diego, CA: Lucent Books, 2001.

Vlack, Don. *Art Deco Architecture in New York, 1920–1940.* New York: Harper and Rowe, 1974.

Wallenchinsky, David. *The Complete Book of the Olympics.* New York: Viking, 1984.

Walters, Brian. *The Illustrated History of Air Travel.* New York: Marshall Cavendish, 1979.

Weisberger, Bernard, A., ed. *The WPA Guide to America: The Best of 1930s America as Seen by the Federal Writers Project.* New York: Pantheon, 1985.

Whitelaw, Nancy. *Margaret Sanger: Every Child a Wanted Child.* New York: Dillon Press, 1994.

Whittingham, Richard. *Rites of Autumn: The Story of College Football.* New York: Free Press, 2001.

Wilson, Charles Reagan, and William Ferris, eds. *Encyclopedia of Southern Culture.* Chapel Hill: University of North Carolina Press, 1989.

Wind, Herbert Warren. *The Story of American Golf.* New York: Callaway Editions, 2000.

Wollstein, Hans J. *Vixens, Floozies and Molls: 28 Actresses of Late 1920s and 1930s Hollywood.* New York: McFarland, 1999.

Woog, Adam. *Gangsters.* San Diego, CA: Lucent Books, 2000.

Woog, Adam. *Roosevelt and the New Deal.* San Diego, CA: Lucent Books, 1998.

Wroble, Lisa. *Kids During the Great Depression.* New York: Powerkids Press, 1999.

Yount, Lisa. *Disease Detectives.* San Diego: Lucent Books, 2000.

Yount, Lisa. *Genetics and Genetic Engineering.* New York: Facts on File, 1997.

Yount, Lisa. *History of Medicine.* San Diego: Lucent Books, 2001.

WEB SITES

America from the Great Depression to World War II: Photographs from the FSA-OWI, 1935–1945. http://memory.loc.gov/ammem/fsahtml/fahome.html (accessed July 23, 2002).

American Architecture—Twentieth Century—1930 to 1939. http://www.great-buildings.com/types/usa/usa_1930–1939.html (accessed July 23, 2002).

American Eugenics Society Scrapbook. http://www.amphilsoc.org/library/exhibits/treasures/aes.htm (accessed July 23, 2002).

American Institute of Physics: Center for History of Physics. http://www.aip.org/history/ (accessed July 23, 2002).

American Red Cross History: 1920–1939. http://www.redcross.org/museum/19201939b.html (accessed July 23, 2002).

The Atomic Century. http://www.dpi.anl.gov/dpi2/timelines/1930s.htm (accessed July 23, 2002).

Blue Cross and Blue Shield History. http://www.bcbs.com/whoweare/history.html (accessed July 23, 2002).

College Football Hall of Fame. http://www.collegefootball.org (accessed July 23, 2002).

Consortium of Vermont Colleges: Bennington. http://www.vtcolleges.org/vtcolleges/benc/ (accessed July 23, 2002).

The Costume Gallery: Women's Fashions 1930s. http://www.costumegallery.com/1930.htm (accessed July 23, 2002).

Cyber Boxing Zone Encyclopedia. http://www.cyberboxingzone.com/boxing/hist-idx.htm (accessed July 23, 2002).

Dirks, Tim. *Greatest Films of the 1930s.* http://www.filmsite.org/30sintro.html (accessed July 23, 2002).

Earthquake Hazards Program: Science of Seismology. http://earthquake.usgs.gov/4kids//science.html (accessed July 23, 2002).

FDR Library and Digital Archives: K12 Learning Center. http://www.fdrlibrary.marist.edu/teach.html (accessed July 23, 2002).

Frank Lloyd Wright Foundation. http://www.franklloydwright.org/ (accessed July 23, 2002).

Great Depression and World War II, 1929–1945: Art and Entertainment in the 1930s and 1940s. Library of Congress: American Memory Timeline. http://memory.loc.gov/ammem/ndlpedu/features/timeline/depwwii/art/art.html (accessed July 23, 2002).

Herbert Hoover Presidential Library. http://hoover.nara.gov/ (accessed July, 2002).

Inaugural Addresses of the Presidents of the United States: Franklin D. Roosevelt, First Inaugural Address, March 4, 1933. http://www.bartleby.com/124/pres49.html (accessed July 23, 2002).

Industrial Designers and Streamlining. http://www.pbs.org/wgbh/amex/streamliners/peoplecvents/p_designers.html (accessed July 23, 2002).

March of Dimes History and Mission. http://www.modimes.org/AboutUs/4220.htm (accessed July 23, 2002).

The National Baseball Hall of Fame and Museum. http://www.baseballhalloffame.org (accessed July 23, 2002).

National Institute of Standards and Technology: The Depression. http://www.100.nist.gov/depression.htm (accessed July 23, 2002).

New Deal Network. http://newdeal.feri.org/ (accessed July, 2002).

The Pharmaceutical Century: 1920s and 1930s. http://pubs.acs.org/journals/pharmcent/Ch2.html (accessed July 23, 2002).

Pro Football Hall of Fame. http://www.profootballhof.com (accessed July 23, 2002).

Schools as Social Regulators, 1920s and 1930s Homepage. http://www.bc.edu/bc_org/avp/soe/te/pages/docstudwork/ed711/pages/regulator1.html (accessed July 23, 2002).

Spartacus Encyclopedia of USA History. http://www.spartacus.schoolnet.co.uk/USA.htm (accessed July 23, 2002).

Student Activism in the 1930s. http://newdeal.feri.org/students/captions.htm (accessed July 23, 2002).

Wofford, Andy. *The Rural South in the 1930s.* http://dsl.snet.net/features/issues/articles/2000/10270101.shtml (accessed July 23, 2002).

Where to Learn More

Index